TO FORESTALL

The Imminent
Super-Depression

AND

Armageddon

TO FORESTALL

The Imminent Super-Depression

AND

Armageddon

BY

JOSEPH E. SHAFER, Ph.D.
Professor Emeritus of Economics
Alaskan Methodist University

The Depression Press
1385 Hymettus Ave.
P. O. Box 2610
Leucadia, CA 92024

Library of Congress Cataloging in Publication Data

ISBN 0-945246-00-5

Printed in U.S.A.

10 9 8 7 6 5 4 3 2 1

Contents

Preface

This work prophesies the coming within the foreseeable future of a super-depression, one far more severe than the Great Depression of the early 1930s. Yet no very exact date is specified herein. Had we continued unchanged to require the ratio of gold in the reserves of our U.S. commercial banks that applied twenty-five years ago, depression likely would have descended upon us many years ago. But with the complete elimination of any requirement of gold in such reserves, with reliance instead simply upon the wisdom and wills of men, we merely have delayed the day of reckoning; that day is made quite uncertain, but not canceled.

Through this last twenty or more years we have been progressively building our financial system into a bigger and bigger and knottier and knottier tangle. Yet the day will come, likely before the turn of the century, when we shall be compelled to try to untangle our mass of knots. The very great danger is that already we have gone so far the free enterprise system world-wide may be unable to survive.

Especially within recent months several other writers and commentators have begun to prophesize the coming of a serious "recession." The fundamental difference between their views and this present one is that herein is set forth the explanation as to why our apparent prosperity has set the stage for a super-depression. In other words, herein is given the diagnosis, the vitally needed diagnosis. And that diagnosis is derived directly from my having pursued for many years, actually several decades, analyses of the exact nature of the primary objective that was evolved automatically and repeatedly by big free enterprise firms, and of the financial institutions that have been generated in connection therewith and the manner of their functioning. Such needed analysis has been overlooked virtually completely in all systems of theory that attempt to explain free enterprise. But if we strive to understand the world's "market systems" fully and objectively theory must be altered to take into account the facts of the actually existing, predominant big business. If we are to have any realistic hope of preserving the several advantages free enterprise does possess, it is essential that we first find the correct diagnosis of our nation's (and the world's) financial ills and therefrom devise treatments that truly are revelant to that valid diagnosis. Successful ministrations must be based, of course, on a correct diagnosis. We hope it is not yet too late to devise for free enterprise some life-saving regimens.

An assertion can be made which should enable most readers to distinguish a vital difference between the foundation of the analyses herein and an assumption underlying, implicitly if not explicitly, every other system of theory that purports to help explain free enterprise. All prior formulations are built on their embracing the primary premise on which Say's Law of Markets is based, namely, the belief that

". . . the income derived in the aggregate by all elements in the community concerned in a productive activity necessarily has a value exactly equal to the *value* of the output."

J. M. Keynes, *The General Theory . . .,* page 20

Keynes (and all others, such as supply-sider George Gilder) interpret the above to mean that the costs and expenses paid out of capital funds by business to persons who help produce goods and services naturally supply to them sufficient money incomes collectively so that they are empowered (if they lay out those funds with ordinary dispatch) to buy and pay for the entire output. But . . . But corporate dividend distributions in fact in the real world are not treated by approved accounting as costs or expenses, and according to corporate law they dare not be paid out of capital funds. Hence the total of the cost and expense payments made by big corporate firms out of their capital funds to compensate the elements in the community concerned in the productive activity aggregate somewhat less than the value (needed selling price) of the output. Such firms in order to be "successful" when selling products require an "add-on" above average costs and expenses to provide an acceptable margin for money profit. The need for and pursuit of money profits as an add-on was a wholly natural evolution as business became large scale. And it was, likely, the sole objective that easily came to mind. In contrast to other systems of theory, the present work is based firmly on the fact that in covering their costs and expenses of production out of their capital funds big corporate firms create incomes for potential buyers that in aggregate are a bit less than sufficient to enable the recipients to purchase the entire output; the selling prices of large corporations must exceed their costs and expenses on the average.

The foregoing discussion should enable the reader to comprehend that the issue clearly now is drawn between this present work and prior systems of theory that have intended to explain free enterprise.

The analyses herein focus on explaining the financial institutions of big firms (those which enjoy $1,000,000 annual revenue or more) which in the last decade have bulked in the U.S.A. to only 2% to 3% of total business ventures. Such firms dominate, since that tiny fraction now takes in fully 75% of the whole of business revenues and employs 75% or more of the workers now holding jobs. (In addition, many small business entities strive to operate in the same ways, financially, as do the huge corporations.) Hence it has become imperative that we, as theorists, now devote adequate and unbiased attention to financial matters about which in the past we have made unreal assumptions and have ignored as a result.

If the predicted super-depression does descend upon us, it is recommended that this present work then be studied with care and objectivity, since it promises to be the sole diagnosis whch can enable us to evolve treatments that will maintain the life of our beloved system. Yet it will be even wiser if we will discipline ourselves into evaluating this work fully and objectively in advance of the depression.

Joseph E. Shafer
San Diego, California, U.S.A.
May 5, 1988

CHAPTER 1

The Urgent Need
For this Summary

This revised but shortened presentation is in fact the epitome of a lifetime of analysis and writing pursued "after hours" beyond regular academic employment and duties. And such research has run somewhat counter to conventional economic theory by delving into matters heretofore unexplored. But because the very survival of our free enterprise system now is threatened, probably is in greater danger than ever before, the insights herein offered are so needed that they very soon must be examined thoroughly and weighed objectively.

It is my hope that we can preserve some of the most fundamental elements of the free enterprise system, for in several crucial ways this system has been and is superior to any alternative ever tried. On the one hand free enterprise in leading developed nations has stimulated inventiveness and innovation that results in very efficient production of want-satisfying goods and services, and where fully developed, it has yielded the highest standards of living ever known. On the other hand, free enterprise is and always has been a close companion to personal freedom and political freedom, freedoms that we humans seem inevitably to cherish. It is my fervent hope that we can develop and install those changes, those medications and/or surgery and/ or therapy that will overcome the afflictions that the free enterprise system suffers. For that purpose relevant diagnosis is imperative.

Free enterprise does suffer some life-threatening afflictions. One is a result of its inheritance, and others developed through the ages because of unenlightened gorging on unhealthy sweets. It is growing ever more clear that the financial health of our system is in jeopardy. Unless we soon institute some treatments developed from the logical application of a truly relevant diagnosis, our private enterprise system likely will succumb from the ailments brought on by the financial malignancies which now weaken it.

This, really an abridgement, is being addressed at the time of its preparation mainly to non-economists who have become concerned about the massive problems that our "economy," and those of numerous friendly nations throughout the world, are encountering. Such non-economist laymen who work to preserve the beneficial parts of our system are asked to study this presentation thoroughly and thoughtfully and thus to strive to prepare themselves for the financial catalysm that will likely overtake us in the next few years if we fail to devise some needed alterations. Those who have attained full qualifications to be regarded as economists are, in general, likely currently to be skeptical of the predictions and analyses offered herein. As long as "economic conditions" have not deteriorated to a completely unacceptable state, nearly all persons thoroughly schooled in economic theory will remain unable to evaluate objectively any unconventional views. They should skim through this epitome (and also the special summary inserted following Chapter 8) in a hasty, but not too superficial way, and then lay it aside for still more carefully objective and more sympathetic examination if and when that life-threatening illness (that super-depression) does overtake free enterprise. Adequate and thoughtful consideration of what is said herein will supply the diagnosis that should enable us to institute indicated treatments and changes that can preserve life and restore health to our system.

The unorthodox (insofar as "Economics" is concerned) analyses summarized herein are offered by one who, in addition to having qualifications to be labeled "an economist," also has become a "chrematist." The words "chrematistics" and "chrematist" are defined in some printings of the second edition of the unabridged Webster's Dictionary. These are words that also came from the ancient Greek, as does "economics." Aristotle used "chrematistics" to refer to the "money-making" objective and processes the merchants in and around the Mediterranean Sea developed in pursuing business. So a "chrematist" is one who studies or analyzes the institutions and processes of money-making. Apparently Aristotle observed that those ancient merchants naturally evolved the drive to "make money." Likewise did international merchants in the centuries following the Crusades. And similarly also have all big businesses (firms engaged in one or more phases of production) in the present era. Because significant divisions of labor, and economies of scale, have come to be the rule in many other aspects of production (including transportation, communication and information storage, and processing, as well as manufacturing, in addition to long-distance international and large-scale merchandising), big business naturally has grown to be dominant in many phases of making as fully as of the marketing of desired goods and services. And all of us know that every big firm that is engaged in one or more phases of production seeks and/or is actually controlled by the aim to make money.

However, few of us as economists, in fact almost none of us, have investigated objectively the exact nature and processes of money-making by big businesses that strive to help satisfy human wants. "Economics," a word derived from the Greek, means household management. We as economists have virtually always confined our investigations and theorizing to household management. We have discussed little except how human wants are satisfied by the production, exchange, and distribution of goods and services, hence the best uses of scarce physical resources. Significant unjustified assumptions usually have been made with respect to the realization of business profits, especially with respect to the need for "minimum, necessary profits"; that idea has enabled theorists to view such profits as a necessary "social cost" and has permitted them to dismiss the matter by letting their minds assume uncritically that somehow they are actual costs. Some additional comments along this line will be found in later chapters.

In fact, few if any economists have seen any need for careful study of the nature of money-making by big producing business organizations. And almost none have qualified themselves for such study by acquiring an adequate knowledge of business accounting and of the law of corporate finance. Yet the majority of all of our so-called "economic" problems are problems of finance, especially of the finance applicable and related to big firms (producing businesses) in their pursuit of money profits.

As will become evident to anyone who goes through the "macro-chrematistics" sketches that follow, weighing them thoroughly and open-mindedly, the nature and causes of our "economic" problems, problems that now seem to be virtually imponderable, are revealingly diagnosed. In point of fact, our current "economic" problems are not "economic problems"; instead, they are "chrematistic problems," financial problems. And until and unless we come to understand them correctly, and attain the truly relevant diagnosis, the danger is that we cannot avoid seeing free enterprise die a miserable death. Correct diagnosis is imperative for successful treatment that will assure survival of our existing system.

(Let it be emphasized that in all that follows reference is to big businesses engaged in producing. None of the subsequent analyses deal with "money-making" via pure speculation, gambling, realizing capital gains, the financial manipulations of "take over," or other "sharp" or questionable manipulations.)

(Chapters 2 through 8 were prepared for non-economist readers. Any reader who is well versed in economic theory may choose to skip to p. 99.)

CHAPTER 2

Prophecies of Some Dire Financial Developments and Some Dire Consequences

Unless we institute quite soon some crucial, but not very disturbing, changes (medications, surgery, or therapy) growing from and truly relative to the cause of the malady our system suffers, we shall witness and experience some highly adverse developments. Our economy, chrematistic institutions and inevitably our political system, as well as the survival of free enterprise and other freedoms kin to free enterprise will be affected. Consider the following:

1. The threat most imminent and most horrible to the average citizen of the U.S. is the probability that this nation will fall victim to a depression in the proximate future. My unhesitating prophesy is that, unless we soon make changes that are relevant to the correct diagnosis, we shall suffer a depression that will be far more severe than any previously known. We have got our

financial affairs into a tangle many times worse than that of the late 1920s. In the absence of changes indicated by correct analysis of big-business's financial systems and their functioning, the forthcoming depression will far exceed that of the early 1930s.

The foregoing prophecy may be taken as a supplement to my article entitled "An Explanation of the Business Cycle," prepared in 1927 and published late in 1928 in a leading periodical specializing in economics. If any reader wishes to review that article, he is asked to evaluate it in terms of a description in advance of what did happen subsequently in The Great Depression and in the light of the far more primitive, even ancient, state of the art in the late 1920s. In 1927, there was yet no "circuit-velocity" concept of money turnover, (which needed formulation I had worked out independently for my own use). There were no *Business Cycles, the Problem and Its Setting* by W.C. Mitchell of the N.B.E.R., no Keynes' *General Theory* . . ., no G.N.P. or Y statistics, and very sparse monetary, credit, or inventory statistics.

My present prophecy does not purport to predict when such a depression will befall this nation and other free enterprise areas that are leaders in fostering big businesses. My chrematistic analysis yields in the main the conclusion that profit making in the macro-chrematistics sense succeeds in causing prosperity for an uncertain span of time as the result of financial expansions that I have labeled as "artificial." There is no particular amount or degree of accumulated expansion which sets a limit beyond which it cannot be carried. Sooner or later, for one reason or another (commonly a psychological reaction such as growing fear), a limit is reached and stagnation sets in. This may be followed by attempts at liquidation, which latter, if extensive, will be true depression.

2. Unless we soon provide changes that are relevant to a correct diagnosis, we shall be able to postpone the coming huge

depression only as long as we continue those financial expansions that eventuate in the kind of profits recorded in the accounts of our big (producing) firms. Reference in particular is to the expansion of the money supply by way of increases in "commercial bank type" credit which gives rise to enlarged money in circulation. That inevitably will cause further "debt-inflation" by enlarging outstanding accumulated debts.

Such money expansions are no longer confined to firms traditionally thought of as "commercial banks." The "NOW" accounts of many thrift institutions have come to function in virtually the same way to create demand-deposit money. When money is created by the kind of lending which adds to demand deposits it inflates debts. Borrowers get deeper into debt, even though prices may not rise correspondingly, or not at all. We suffered such inflation in 1873 to 1890 and again from 1923 to 1929 while prices moved along level (that is, sideways) or declined a bit. Our choice among evils here in the U.S. is to suffer depression and liquidation relatively soon or to inflate debts (perhaps with prices being little changed) via continued growth of our money supply through "commercial banking" operations, thus to build our financial tangles up to an even markedly bigger letdown later.

Our rapidity of inflating, in the sense of expanding credit and getting borrowers more and more deeply into debt, has taken a quantum jump during these last two decades. We in the U.S. thought we had grown wise enough to remove, in the mid-1960s and early 1970s, all ties of commercial bank deposits and of bank notes (i.e., Federal Reserve Notes) to any reserves of precious metals. If these restrictions had not been removed, undoubtedly we would have encountered limits some time past. However, removal of any such restraints has enabled us to rush along at a faster pace. We are building up debts and putting off any reckoning until a later time as we set ourselves for a much greater plunge.

3. If we strive valiantly to reduce the deficit of the federal government in a truly meaningful way (not simply to provide a minor, token reduction) by cutting expenditures, we shall bring on the forthcoming depression speedily, unless we first provide relevant changes such as characterized in the first paragraph of this chapter. Curtailment of U.S. overspending will yield, as an early result of such budget-balancing, a reduction in the rate of expansion of those financial processes. Such processes are, as will be shown in later chapters, vital to the generation and continuation of prosperity for our big producing firms.

In the absence of relevant changes in our profits-yielding institutions and processes, we cannot balance that budget nor reduce the annual deficit significantly by increasing greatly the collection of taxes, either. If we continue to incur huge deficits (while our financial institutions remain unaltered) we shall experience virtually runaway inflation sooner or later. We will then deflate into a still bigger depression.

4. If we fail to make changes, indicated by a full and correct understanding of the overall financial profit-making institutions and processes of big (producing) firms, the debts and money problems of a number of U.S. farmers likely will culminate before long in great losses, both to farmers and to the banking organizations as creditors. Many bank failures, with large aggregate losses, will follow.

5. Unless we provide alterations to the profits-yielding techniques of our large-sized firms engaged in producing, it's likely that we, as well as people in other leading business nations, will continue to treat the less economically developed areas of the free world as our colonies, as leading nations did in the colonial

period of modern history. Our methods have changed, at least have grown far more subtle, but the objective and effects remain almost identical to what is regarded as a past period. As a result, it will prove impossible for those "colonies" and their nationals to pay (or for us to collect) debts which are now relatively huge. Consider our Latin American neighbors, who currently owe many hundreds of billions of dollars, in large part to banks in the U.S., and smaller amounts to banks in other leading free enterprise nations. If they are to pay off both principal and interest on a reasonable time schedule, they can do so only by practicing great austerity. They must export more (working harder to increase their output) and import less. Each of these will lower their average standards of living, especially of their common people. This often leads to revolution, with the revolutionists striving to institute communism (seeing no other choice apart from the free enterprise system that has been oppressing them).

Since their paying off both principal and interest will seem impossible and even unwise, how about actually paying the interest to keep the debts "performing" in the eyes of the creditors? That will require the same kind of austerity on the part of the common people of those debtor nations, even if on a smaller scale. Their people, as a whole, will be required to curtail consumption as they export more and import less.

Another alternative is to induce the creditors, mostly commercial banks, to reschedule the interest due and add that to the accumulated debt, thus making the total larger but for a time preventing default. Yet, this simply puts off the day of reckoning.

Other alternatives are for the creditor banks to "write off" (gradually) much of those "non-performing" foreign debts and take their losses or, instead, to sell some of those debts at more or less discount to others who might stand willing to buy, and hope to hold reductions as small as possible.

However, there is a bit more to this whole matter. If any debtor nation does succeed in getting away with sufficient austerity on the parts of its average citizens, does increase exports and reduce imports, there will be detriment felt in those leading business nations whose exports will be trimmed and whose demand for domestically produced goods will be diminished. Great unavoidable disturbances will be experienced at both ends.

Moreover, the lending banks will be forced eventually to take losses on much of the foreign debts they hold as assets. This may cause many bank failures and precipitate the forthcoming depression, including severe liquidations in all financial aspects of our system.

Let attention be focused briefly again on the less-developed areas of the free world. They continue to be treated like colonies because of the natural objective and methods evolved by our big business firms. The principal method has changed fundamentally and now is far more subtle than during what is called the Mercantilistic Period of modern history. However, the results today are equally adverse. Because of greater subtlety, the advantage of the rich nations over the poor may be more detrimental to the latter group. The growth of interdependence may have made more pervasive those bad effects.

6. It seems logical to mention briefly the huge "trade deficit" which we in the U.S. have been suffering from for some time. Especially now in the 1980s, it appears that certain countries (including our main enemies during World War II) have turned the table on us. Further, the OPEC nations have been adding to our woes by their collective actions.

Analyses presented here to explain how the drive of our big producer firms and big exporter firms to "make money" have been countered by the U.S. workers' insistence on higher wages (easily met by artificial expansion of the money supply to provide the additional required "working capital" to validate such increased costs) often have rendered industries unable to compete with many ventures such as in West Germany and in Japan. It will not be possible to discover needed changes to cure much of our trade deficit until we first understand correctly and fully the nature of profit-making by big producing businesses and the institutions that have evolved in connection therewith.

Both the Japanese and OPEC members find themselves in an unusual position. They, from their point of view, can continue to realize favorable trade balances indefinitely as long as the U.S. dollar remains strong and as long as investments somewhere in the U.S. seem secure and offer high yields. Both the Japanese and Middle East citizens and governments find it attractive to buy up or build properties, enterprises, and government debt in the United States.

So our purchases in the U.S. of great quantities of foreign rather than domestic products tend to curtail any significant inflation of our prices. Conversely, they maintain prosperity in a few friendly countries, such as Japan and West Germany. Should we succeed in "correcting" our trade imbalance in one way or another while our profits-generating institutions remain unchanged, we shall cause great depression in those areas that have been in recent years able to sell us goods of far greater total value than those they buy from us. Our considerable expansion of our money supply has tended to yield them prosperity and great benefit. If we cease functioning in this manner, they will suffer greatly, economically and financially.

7. Equally ominous for continued prosperity here in the U.S., if we fail to make some changes consistent with the correct diagnosis of our financial ills revealed by the realistic understanding of money-making pursued by big producing firms, is the recent growth and accumulation of outstanding consumer debts. Consumers' installment debts have been piling up since the beginning of 1984 at the rate of 20% per year. In mid-1985, they

totaled approximately $500 billion. This process was really "invented" in the early 1920s. When the Great Depression struck in 1929 the consumer debt aggregated to about $7.25 billion. Now the amount outstanding is around seventy (70) times as big, and ballooning. If the present rate of increase continues, installment credit outstanding here in this nation will climb to approximately $1 trillion by the end of 1988. Even if the continued growth is at the same dollar volume per year as since the end of 1983, the $1 trillion total will be reached within seven years from date of writing, from 1985.

Should we strive to collect any significant amount of outstanding consumer installment debt, or even curtail its high-rate ballooning, we shall curtail the retail sales that concurrently will be made. Even the heading off of further significant expansion, or stopping of its continued breakneck ballooning, will impair whatever sales-prosperity might have been experienced. Serious reduction of the outstanding total already attained must cause a decline in whatever prosperity there may be. It will likely precipitate strenuous attempts at collection, leading to further liquidation, to significantly reduced current retail sales, and to severe depression.

There is a temptation to bring into this analysis a discussion of the expansion of the non-installment debt of consumers. Some decades past it was easy to find useful data reporting estimates of total credit extended and held by retailers. In recent years, such estimates have become hard to obtain. If the credit extended to consumers and held undiscounted by retailers has been growing in amounts and rates corresponding to those of installment credit, they could add appreciably to the totals in this data. It just may be, however, that with the use of bank credit cards in making many small retail credit purchases, the consumer "credit" extended and held undiscounted has increased but little or even has declined.

8. A number of analysts have expressed the view that high

interest rates on home mortgages, on "variable-rate" mortgages, and on mortgages in which home buyers were enticed by initially low interest rates scheduled to rise in later years, will bring great financial hardship for both borrowers and lenders. If home prices and prices in general cease to continue the rises that were expected by both parties, defaults on mortgages could add markedly to our financial woes as we start a big economic and financial decline. Permit me to be a bit hesitant in offering such a specific prophesy here.

9. Additionally, wage rates in many big producing firms in the U.S. have got out of line with those in areas with which we compete in turning out many products that can be shipped readily. Our firms of this type, in pursuing altogether naturally the money-making objective (marking prices on output up reasonably above all money costs) have tried to sell, often using "high pressure" methods, to laborers the latter's share at prices beyond the purchasing power those workers have received. Firms have held back a portion of output or have enticed such potential buyers into debt. Unions in turn have demanded wage increases, frequently pressing through strikes, and boosted wages higher, step by step. Until we make some changes in the business, financial, and profit-pursuing processes, we shall continue to experience justified labor dissatisfaction. We shall continue to have wage rates that are above that level needed to restore us to full international competitiveness. U.S. employment will continue to stagnate while unemployment will fuel the adverse reaction our financial system otherwise cannot avoid. More and more of those rapidly growing consumer debts before long will begin to be defaulted, as will debts owed by foreign nations and nationals, and by our farmers.

In many of our old-line "smoke-stack" industries in which a small number of firms exists and costs, especially labor costs, have risen and risen and risen in pursuit of continuous price boosts, we must return to international competitiveness. This will happen only if (1) there are wage concessions or (2) there are significant wage rate increases in competing areas (e.g., Japan) or (3) we succeed in seriously outstripping others in installing robots and automation cutting deeply present unit costs of producing.

10. A few observations here are directed to inflation and deflation themselves. Unless we devise and install a few minimal changes indicated by the correct description of our free enterprise institutions and their manner of functioning, we shall continue to suffer inflation in order to realize prosperity. This does not mean that prices will always be rising if we are to be "prosperous." They did not rise between 1873 and 1890 or between 1923 and 1929. It does mean that we shall rush along increasing the money supply, through expansion of commercial bank loans, and entice various groups of borrowers to fall deeper and deeper into debts. Eventually, when we try to liquidate to some extent, many debtors will find they cannot pay. The thing to watch is the rate of growth, the annual growth rather than the short-term fluctuations, in the outstanding money supply. These days as long as the true money supply continues to grow markedly, big producing firms will show significant profits. But we shall be getting borrowers deeper and deeper into debt.

A modern technique that augments, reinforces, and assures (for a time) that the inflation will rush on faster and faster is "indexation." We virtually "index" the rise in money wage rates by tying the latter to consumer price rises. That tends to validate prior price increases and almost makes inevitable subsequent rise of costs and of prices again in the next period. The process comes to be repeated continuously and sets up a vicious circle. Indexation of other kinds of incomes, such as pensions, tends to make sure that marked-up prices can be realized as they go higher and higher, period by period. Since nearly runaway inflation is made certain, it naturally leads to unbearable financial difficulties in a few years. Indexation means that prices marked above all financial costs (to bring money profits) will be validated. They will require creation and insertion of added money.

The sole kind of full indexation that can be justified is that which operates to keep tax collections in check. Hence, it helps to prevent government expenditures from getting completely out of hand. However, one can justify in the name of morality, equity, and right some indexation of personal income of low or modest size. It is suggested that indexing be limited to a fraction, perhaps not over two-thirds of the rise in prices.

11. Let these sketches of our late-1980s financial tangles be concluded by noting that a number of our banks, both those classified as thrift institutions and those described as commercial banks, are reported to be in shaky and uncertain condition. Some managed with complete honesty have encountered the souring of numerous loans that on origination were thought to be sound by everyone. Other loans were made by bankers who seemed to think that the U.S. government could be counted upon to bail them out if unduly high interest loans of questionable security were made in excessive amounts to friendly governments, especially in Latin America. Further, because of the high interest tradition, many banks have pushed hard to increase their share of the installment and credit-card lending. Still other of our "unit" banks here in the U.S. have suffered because bankers have tried to be "good fellows" in helping to support their communities and friends and businesses, including farmers. Finally, a few banks have been badly or too aggressively managed while a small number have fallen victims to fraud and embezzlement.

Indeed, some of the several difficulties described early in this chapter have come naturally to be focused on our banks. The resulting unsoundness and ill effects will be concentrated initially on the financial debacle and depression that will overtake our free enterprise, capitalistic system before long in the absence of some changes soon.

For the thrill of offering a guess and observing how badly it works out, my prediction is that our downward slide financially will have begun on Sunday, July 28, 1985, when newly elected Alan Garcia Perez was inaugurated as President of Peru. However, Alan Garcia will not be to blame in the slightest degree. His inauguration speech has set the stage for billions, tens of billions, even hundreds of billions of dollars owed by our less developed Latin American neighbor nations, mainly to our big U.S. commercial banks, to *begin* falling into default. Our own federal government, with its great accumulated debt and unresolved huge deficit, is no longer in position to come to the rescue of those banks. Further, the F.D.I.C. (even with the aid of the F.S.L.I.C.) is too small to make more than a minor dent in the financial problems that will eventuate.

If default on the debts of Latin American nations does not precipitate the forthcoming depression, any one of the several other financial snarls mentioned promises to spark the conflagration.

Either before a financial debacle occurs or shortly afterward, we shall find it necessary to alter what we know as commercial banking in some fundamental ways if free enterprise is to survive. Those changes might not prove to be very onerous if we change as little as necessary in the light of the realistic diagnosis. And those organizations known in the past as "thrift institutions" should be required to be returned to their historic operations, those prior to the 1960s, exclusively.

It is one of my most fervent hopes that none of the adverse predictions set forth is, in the short run, a self-fulfilling prophecy. Indeed it would please me greatly if none of them ever material-izes. But that is extremely improbable. My real hope is that we shall have sufficient time and foresight to perfect the diagnosis and therefrom derive the indicated changes in the financial institutions of free enterprise to the end that we shall be able to preserve through the coming centuries those particularly good and beneficial elements of this system of ours. Some very clear-cut, yet not too onerous, changes are required to enable free enterprise to survive.

CHAPTER 3

The Greatest Mistake
In Economic Theory
(Life Threatening
to Free Enterprise)

"It is . . . a proposition which is indubitable, namely that the incomes derived in the aggregate by all elements in the community concerned in a productive activity necessarily has a value exactly equal to the *value* of the output."
J.M. Keynes, The General Theory . . ., p. 20

It is possible to identify exactly and conclusively the single most important mistake ever and always made in economics, since the initial and underlying duty of economic analysis is to explain correctly and make understandable the reality of that which does exist. If the full and accurate disclosure of reality is taken as the basic test, then the true cause of the premier falsity in economics is easy to identify.

Economic theory descriptive of free enterprise, throughout

its history (since 1776), has been completely mistaken because of the creation of and tenacious adherence to the *first* of the two assumptions that together make up "Say's Law of Markets." "Say's Law" was enunciated very early in the 1800s as J.B. Say, a Frenchman, strove to make more orderly, logical, explicit, and popular what he understood Adam Smith to have said in his ... *Wealth of Nations*. The "Law" can be summarized as follows: As we specialize in making things and trading some portion of our output for some output of our neighbors, we are simply trading goods and services for other goods and services. We buy other things we want by using the money we get for things we sell. It alleges that demand is supply and supply is demand. Money serves simply as a facilitating intermediary, a medium of exchange. Demand is always equal to supply. Money can be dropped out of the analysis for ready generalization. There cannot be general overproduction.

When money is used as a medium of exchange, as it has been for many centuries in all but the most primitive economies, and is the growing practice as any society develops, Say's Law supposedly applies; but it does so only because two assumptions are made.

(1) On one hand, *Say's Law* necessarily implies that in a money economy the money incomes that are created for potential buyers in connection with producing (marketing as well as making) are equal to the total of the prices of the aggregate output (the latter impliedly all for sale). Potential buyers are assumed to be paid enough money so that if they promptly spend (or invest) it all, they can purchase the output offered on the market.

(2) On the other hand, *Say's Law* assumes that all such incomes will be spent (and/or invested) without undue delay. Say himself reasoned that rises and falls in interest rates would cause all savings to be "invested" in reasonable course. If no serious

external friction arises, markets would tend naturally to be cleared. That Law did, as later interpreted, provide that there might be "unbalanced production," too much of some things and too little of other products, so markets might not clear properly.

It was not until 1935, about a century and one-third after the work of J.B. Say first was published, that any economist first really questioned, in whole or in part, the fundamental validity of his Law. In 1935, J.M. Keynes in his *General Theory* . . . denied the validity of the *second* of the assumptions that necessarily compose that Law. As the result of Keynes' theorizing about the Great Depression (plus his use of the "new," in the 1920s, concept of "circuit velocity" as the relevant money circulation or turnover in the process of creating money incomes), he advanced the view that because with progress consumers in leading nations usually will receive money incomes that rise gradually and interest rates will gradually decline and yield less and less reward from investing, there is some advantage (lower risk of possible loss) in one's having some liquid funds. Progressively potential buyers will simply hold "liquid" more and more of savings out of their incomes. He asserted that *Say's Law* was mistaken because with progress, he reasoned, more and more of money incomes would be held in diverse liquid forms, neither spent nor invested. His conclusions about "too much savings" was followed soon by recommendations originated by some disciples for "pump priming" via deficit spending. This would restore to the money circulation the equivalent of what savings were theorized to be withdrawn and held liquid.

Let every reader make sure that he understands that Keynes did embrace and take as one of his analytical "givens" that underlying or primary premise of Say's, his unquestioned belief that the money payments naturally made in the course of financing production necessarily create sufficient money incomes for potential buyers; those in total will equal the prices of the whole output. This can be shown beyond doubt by interpreting the final words of the sentence that begins on line 20 of page 20 of Keynes' *General Theory* . . . Any skeptical reader should ponder those thirty (30) words, quoted on p. 21. Keynes must be regarded as the original and leading "demand sider"; he adopted without question Say's *primary premise*.

With respect to "supply siders" it is equally clear that they adopt in their thinking an identical concept. It contends that the financing of production necessarily creates incomes in aggregate that match the total selling prices of the whole output, that underlying first premise imperative in *Say's Law*. This can be established beyond question by a careful study of the last full paragraph on page 47 of George Gilder's 1981 *Wealth and Poverty*, quoted herein on p. 102.

The "supply siders" do not differ at all from the "demand siders" about whether or not potential buyers receive sufficient total money incomes as a result of the financing of production. All systems of economic theory relative to free enterprise since J.B. Say have assumed that these income recipients do. In the last fifty years, the Keynesian followers have been reasoning that there may be too much savings followed by some potential purchasing power being withdrawn from the markets and held liquid. In contrast, the "supply side" theorists believe in the trickle-down theory; they hold that we need not worry about too much savings, some of which might come to be withheld from circulation by being held liquid.

However, the truth is that all such schools of economic theory are fundamentally mistaken, each and every one of them, when tested against reality. When we reach a correct analysis of the big firms engaged in producing, the money-making objective they naturally have evolved, and the institutions that have been devised to enable such business organizations to realize profits (which naturally have become controlling), the incomes created fall short of being sufficient. By far the most important concept must be that in highly developed producing areas, large firms ("capitalistic" in the sense of needing much capital funds) naturally arise in most important lines of production. Such firms, in order to "make money," must succeed on the average in selling at prices that exceed the money incomes they naturally create through meeting costs and expenses in connection with their output. The greatest mistake in economics theorizing about free enterprise is the speciousness of that underlying, primary premise on which *Say's Law* necessarily has to be erected. Cost and expense payments made by big producers fall short of equaling the aggregate asking prices of the output, the desired "margin for profit" being the difference, the shortfall in total incomes created.

Responsibility for the great mistake that was "set in concrete" in *Say's Law* was not that of J.B. Say alone. The Mercantilistic writers, some of whom antedated Say by many decades and even centuries, did a very imperfect job of explaining the "business system" that the great merchants unwittingly had evolved. Adam Smith's . . . *Wealth of Nations* was in some respects far too narrow to treat adequately the then existing realities of the naturally evolving business financial system. When we analyze fully and objectively the rise and growth of the financial operations of the leading merchants in western Europe between the Crusades and the 1776 publication date of Smith's original work, we find that several notions in the . . . *Wealth of Nations* require alteration in order to treat reality. We find that the underlying premise on which *Say's Law* is built will have to be discarded. Let attention be focused on Smith's 1776 book.

In differing from the French "school" of Physiocrats, with some members of which he had visited while traveling in France, Adam Smith originated the view that it is labor, rather than nature, which is productive. Accordingly, he developed the view that the great advance in productivity and per capita output is the result of division of labor. Indeed he originated the analytical principle of division of labor. It is this idea that he championed most in his first chapter, entitled "Of Division of Labor." That description of division of labor is satisfactory — as far as he goes in his Chapter

I. But one distracting fault is that it falls short. It does not go far enough.

There are two refinements required on Smith's treatment of division of labor in order to bring his basic concept abreast of full reality. On the one hand, Smith's notion of what should be classified as division of labor seems to be much too narrow. He apparently reasoned that the principle applies only to the creation of form utility, the making of things in agriculture (cultivation and/or husbandry), or by handicraft or more complex manufacture such as pin-making. Economists have, subsequently and correctly, broadened the scope of that which must be encompassed in the concept of "production" to include the creation of time utility, place utility, and ownership utility. Physical things that are turned out under the full potential advantages of division of labor require to be marketed. Smith devoted his first two chapters to describing and lauding division of labor in manufacturing specifically in his portrayal of ten men working at some eighteen different operations to turn out collectively "upwards of forty-eight thousand" straight pins in a day. In his third chapter, he explained that "the Division of Labor Is Limited by the Extent of the Market." In that early chapter he did discuss land transport by use of horses and great wagons and, in contrast, water transport between ports, via ships. He pointed out that the latter is far more efficient and less expensive. He did use the word "expence" several times and asserted that the "expence" of transport directly falls upon the price of the goods transported. When one has embraced the idea that the creation of time and place and ownership utilities also are production, the very first division of labor in producing must have been either the ownership and operation of transport facilities, such as ships used in commerce, or alternatively, the appearance of persons operating specifically as traders or merchants. Whichever of those two came first, division of labor antedated by many centuries, both in the modern era and in and around the Mediterranean Sea in ancient western civilization, the making of straight pins as described by Adam Smith.

On the other hand, Smith's concept of division of labor is a bit too broad. It appears to include economic activity which, to my mind, might better be described simply as individual or household "specialization." Specialization of economic activities surely must have arisen very early in human existence. Within the family it seems correct to believe that almost from the beginning members naturally came to specialize in the dividing up of the their diverse tasks of getting a living and maintaining life. This includes one or more members going hunting, fishing, or "going to war" while other family members worked at home. As long as tasks are divided up simply among household members, including any apprentices, it seems better to think for analysis' sake in terms of "specialization." Such specialization includes the task of taking to market surplus output which the household desires to trade for specialties turned out by other households. Such trades can be either by barter or by way of "money," a commodity used as a medium. It seems to me that "specialization" remains the more accurate term so long as money is not being used as capital funds and is not required to be paid out to meet costs and expenses to finance production. Hence, we should use "division of labor" to refer to situations in which money capital funds are collected together and used to pay costs and expenses of production.

Had Adam Smith followed his notation of the crucial need for markets and for efficient and cheap transport, and included in production the creation of the marketing utilities (time and place and ownership) along with creation of form utility, he surely might have gone on to develop several concepts essential to understanding big business which was even then engaged in form utility creation. Such needed concepts include:

1. Several steps, one of which is marketing, are inevitably

required for completed production of anything that entails significant division of labor that almost always requires big size in an organization to realize in full the economies of scale potential.

2. Every case of significant division of labor in producing a physical good involves several steps that are, of course, time-consuming, so that the virtually inevitable use of money to pay business costs and expenses creates a circuit flow or income circulation of money because money must move backward against the forward flow of output. Since cost and expenses are paid *quid pro quo* (although some payments are made in advance and some afterwards), the flows in the two opposite directions are timed mutually by each other. Sometimes one flow sets the pace and some-times the pace is set by the other. Money moves with a circuit velocity virtually identical to the speed of the counter flow of output.

3. In order for big producer firms to meet costs and expenses, they must raise money to use as capital funds, from which "costs" are incurred for such things as plant and equipment and "expenses" for such things as materials, labor, and power. Such entrepreneurs pay out money to cover costs and expenses and expect to recover or replenish such money capital funds through sales.

4. The large producing enterprises almost always require so much capital funds that there comes to be "absentee ownership." In absentee ownership, the money used as capital funds is often furnished by individuals who do not serve either as workers or as active, day-to-day managers. Even firms that start small with owners actively partici-pating often become essentially only absentee-owned as the enterprise grows larger and larger, or as age eventuates in retirement, or as death transfers the ownership of capital funds to heirs.

5. Whenever the free enterprise division of labor results in separated creation of marketing utilities with capital funds being used to pay costs and expenses both of the making and of the marketing, money's income-creating circulation moving counter to the flow of output but at the same speed, the entrepreneurs involved naturally evolve the money-making objective or adopt it from prior pattern-setters. The intention here is to emphasize the naturalness of embracing that objective. Efficient operation requires the making of payments out of money capital funds followed usually by the sale of output to recover money again. It naturally comes about that the business sellers strive to obtain more money through sales than what is paid out as costs and expenses attributable to the items sold. Indeed this is so natural that the matter can be put in the form of a challenge to any reader who is skeptical. State if you can some other reasonable objective that might be pursued instead.

Each of the above five concepts describes an element of what long had been established reality by the time Smith wrote his ... *Wealth of Nations* in the ten years up to 1776. The merchants naturally began to reappear shortly after the Crusades as they also naturally had evolved in ancient western civilization prior to the Dark Ages. Concurrently, large-scale ship transport had continued its development so strongly that some historians speak of the "Commercial Revolution" as having taken place in the fourteenth and fifteenth centuries. Obviously the great merchants as they reappeared found it necessary to acquire money to use as capital funds. This money was used to cover at minimum the cost of some physical capital equipment and of merchandise stock-in-trade plus the expenses of transport and the wages and sometimes the "keep" of employees who aided in transporting, storing, selling, and delivering the goods. If by land transport, expenses sometimes included such items as tolls and taxes and kindred charges. Undoubtedly money funds were often obtained by borrowing from others, relatives and friends, or by "selling" shares in the venture. Without doubt some capital funds were raised from "absentee owners."

Similar observations are required about transport of goods by water. Some individual or group had to own a ship even if only one ship was involved. Likely that person, household, or group did not build the ship; instead the owner almost always had to collect the money funds to pay for its construction, so the ship became a cost to the venturer(s). Correspondingly, in order to operate the ship, the owner(s) had to buy provisions for it and hire sailors to man it. The latter required some money wages as well as "keep" while aboard ship. Disbursements of money capital funds undoubtedly were essential to finance the costs and expenses of owning and operating a single ship. Hence it was natural to expect to recover reimbursement funds by collecting money in exchange for the service rendered. If the shipping venture prospered, the same individual or group would try to expand the service to include the ownership and operation of several vessels. Most of these vessels were manned entirely by "hired hands," both officers and seamen, so "absentee owner- ship" was involved.

Finally, ponder Smith's illustration of division of labor in what he characterizes as the "trifling manufacture," in a work- house equipped with some few simple items of capital equipment, of 48,000 pins in a day by ten men sharing some eighteen different tasks. Some one or more persons had to provide the workplace and the simple tools and machinery required. As the ten pin-makers undoubtedly did not build the factory, its construction was paid for by someone who supplied the money funds required. Someone must have supplied additional capital funds to cover the cost of the wire which was the basic material. The wire, itself, was necessarily the product of mining, iron and steel-making, and wire-pulling. The expenses of operating the "workhouse" such as the wages and the charges for power and light and heat used would have to be provided. It is most unlikely that the output of 200 "papers of pins" per day or 1200 "papers of pins" per week (my guess, checking having proved impossible, is that there are some 240 pins to the "paper") surely was not simply divided up among the ten workers.Undoubtedly the output was sold in job-lots for money and then passed on through normal marketing steps. At each step money capital is disbursed and then replenished via sales. Transporting and merchandising became involved in the division of labor sequence, as had the mining of materials and the manufacture of wire had to antedate the actual making of the pins.

Indeed, Smith's comments show that he saw the operations of the great merchants prominently about him and observed their evolved institutions and operations including the money-making objective embodied in the natural business drive to sell goods for more money than laid out as costs and expenses. At various spots in his book he remarked upon the merchants "buying to sell again," "buying to sell with a profit," their striving always to "buy cheap and sell dear," and their perceived need for making a "reasonable profit." Let one ponder this his most colorful assertion, "The merchants and artificers . . . acted merely from a view of their own interest, and in pursuit of their own peddlar principle of turning a penny wherever a penny was to be got" (Adam Smith . . . *Wealth of Nations,* Sterling and Slade, Edinburgh, 1819, Vol. II, p. 196). Clearly the leading merchants were buying and selling goods. They were using money as capital. They were striving to sell on the average for more money than costs and expenses. Moreover, Smith was observant enough to include "artificers."

Being a professor of moral philosophy, reacting as less than a true scientist, Smith decided that those operations of the merchants were evil, apparently the result of their selfish or evil intentions. He hoped, therefore, that such operations by the merchants and artificers would be eradicated.

He hoped also to witness the eradication of business corporations which he viewed as evil because of their reduction of competition. However, the truth is that realization of the full benefits of division of labor and the resulting economies of scale required the raising and using of large sums of capital funds. Hence some form of organization about like corporations was unavoidable, and the disbursement of money capital funds by producing firms to meet costs and expenses in order to carry on production made the pursuit of money-making altogether natural. This was possibly the only objective that readily could be thought up.

In view of the realities described in the five concepts listed above, Smith ought never to have presented his too simplistic, even archaic, description of the origin and use of money as he did in his Chapter IV. Immediately following his first two chapters descriptive of the division of labor and its great benefits, his third chapter explains that division of labor is limited by the extent of the market. There follows the fourth chapter purporting to explain the origin of money and particularly its "use." He ought to have made "use" plural. His explanation of the use of money progresses only far enough to describe its serving as a medium of exchange to overcome the difficulties of direct barter of things. That pertains to business operations no more complex than those engaged in on market day in a medieval town in western Europe where one or more members of each household specializing in agriculture or handicraft bring in surplus products to trade with one another. No mention is made by Smith of the fact that the then existing merchants and a number of artificers, then moving rapidly to reap the benefits of widening resort to division of labor being realized from some of the great inventions, and the owners of ships engaged in commerce necessarily had to use money as capital funds. Naturally, both groups turned to trying to make money by selling their goods or services for more money than they had paid out to cover costs and expenses.

To be sure, Smith later in his work, particularly in Chapter II of Book II, discussed money further. He included the rise of banking and the issuing of bank notes, which he regarded simply as lower-cost substitutes for metal coins, for use as medium of exchange. Several times in that chapter, he mentioned "the great wheel of circulation." However, the whole of Chapter II of Book II admits of no interpretation other than that he conceived of money as being used solely as a medium of exchange to overcome the difficulties of bartering of things for things.

Had Adam Smith recognized the fact that many merchants really were using money as capital funds, were making payments to meet costs and expenses, that money actually circulated counter to the forward movement of goods through the steps of production resulting from division of labor, that money moves through a circuit with a velocity the same as the pace at which goods flow, that those enterprises that pay out money from their capital funds almost inevitably come naturally to require more money from sales than their costs and expenses, J.B. Say could not have distilled from . . . *The Wealth of Nations* the underlying, primary assumption in his *Law*. That specious primary assumption presumes that the incomes created in connection with financing production are always equal in their total to the aggregate value of the output of products.

In 1868, Karl Marx in *Das Kapital* set forth a recognition of the fact that money is being used by entrepreneurial employers as capital funds. He found that such capitalists, as large-scale merchants and large-scale artificers and ship owners, use money to pay costs and expenses and succeed, if they succeed, by selling their output of goods or services for *more* money. This is made clear in the fourth chapter of *Das Kapital* where he has specified that the original sequence in the use of money was C — M — C.

This anagram symbolizes that money is simply an intermediary, a medium of exchange of commodities for commodities. In time, with the appearance of traders and shipowners giving their full attention to commerce that sequence is transformed into M — C — M', in which traders use money as capital funds and pay out money to cover their costs and expenses. They then strive to acquire money again in making sales. He stated specifically that the "prime" mark placed on the final M is to signify that the end of his sequence must eventuate in more money recovered than disbursed in the first M. Marx did not have or develop, on the one hand, the concept of the circular flow of money. He quite illogically tried to explain money-making in terms of the beloved "labor theory of value" of the Classicists. So he contended, quite mistakenly, that although a product costs an employer only the worth of the *labor embodied*, the product has a money value almost equal to the worth of the *labor saved* the buyer. The former is smaller because of the economies of scale flowing from division of labor. However, in a quick criticism of Marx, the reader should note that the making of money considered collectively must be explained in *financial* and *money* terms , not in labor terms. There is a circular flow of money with its circuit velocity the same as the velocity of production. Despite the irrelevance and fallacy in his use of the two aspects of the labor theory of value to explain how business makes money in the financial sense, and the unavailability to him of the circular flow of money concept, Marx reasoned and asserted that money is used as capital funds and business success is contingent upon sale of output for more money than money costs.

In the first four decades of the twentieth century, the dissenting school of economists known as Institutionalists, started by Thorstein Veblen and including J.R. Commons and W.C. Mitchell, pointed out that big firms (necessary to realize the full economies of scale possible from thorough-going division of labor in numerous lines of production) naturally eventuated in the need for so much money as capital funds to make "absentee ownership" the norm naturally to be expected. The three Institutionalists specified that the institutions of business were what had been overlooked in the analyses of orthodox economics. The institutions and their functioning had to be studied to provide the needed correction to existing theory. Commons recommended that anyone intending to specialize as an economist should begin by devoting thorough study to business finance because any firm's "margin for profit" is its crucial concern. Mitchell wrote that it is correct "to take business profits as the clue to business cycles." Moreover, Veblen observed a vital difference between "economic value" and "pecuniary value." This observation led Mitchell, a graduate student of Veblen's, to distinguish between "making goods" and "making money." However, all three of those leaders came up short of the goal they had specified. Probably the greatest roadblock standing in their path was the lack of the concept of the reality that money flows in a circle through many steps against the forward flow of products. It has a circuit velocity the same as the step-by-step flow of output. Since the V and V' symbols of money velocity, used by Irving Fisher in his famous "equation of exchange" published in 1911, simply stand for an archaic "transaction turnover" concept of money being used only in exchanging finished items (really household product that involves no money costs to producers), any analyst using them will find himself lost in endeavoring to fathom the overall financial operations of big producing business organizations.

Through the 1930s, Mitchell continued to reason in terms of the transaction turnover of money. He believed money able to circulate completely at a faster or slower rate depending solely on the actions and habits of consumers, unrelated to the flow of products. Therefore he could persist in his belief that business cycles are caused by "the backward art of spending money," because consumers during some periods illogically spend too much, followed eventually by a period in which they illogically spend too little.

It was not until in the 1920s, a century and a half after publication of . . . *The Wealth of Nations*, that the concept of the circular flow of money creating income as it passes into and through the hands of potential buyers of end-products, with a circuit velocity matching that of the flow of output, appeared in economic literature. It came first in D.H. Robertson's little book on *Money* and a bit later in the three volumes published by The Brookings Institution, prepared by researchers there, *America's Capacity to Produce, America's Capacity to Consume*, and *The Formation of Capital*. With this development of our insights, we as specialized analysts attained the last of the essential elements that can enable us to understand the system of business that naturally evolved, unwittingly, as the counterpart of the full blossoming of division of labor in the production of things.

To be sure, this last element and concept is related to one more, namely, the realization that marketing functions are necessarily part of production. The creation of time, place, and ownership utilities must be included in the production of things. This is so self-evident and recognition is of such long standing that no attention needs to be devoted here to ascertaining when and by whom the marketing activities and the utilities they create were first inserted into economic theory.

In summary: The following facts and the concepts describing them surely are now made clear.

1. Those who concentrate in performing marketing functions are producing, too.

2. Producing, especially of physical goods, is a time-consuming flow that is matched by a counter flow of money payments, the two having the same velocities, timed by each other.

3. Money is used as capital funds by nearly all enterprises engaged in producing. Often great sums of money are required to meet costs and expenses, especially if they are "great" manufacturers, "great" merchants, or "great" shipping firms. Size is determined by what is required to take full advantage of division of labor and economies of scale.

4. As the organization often must be huge in order to be of top efficiency, the large amount of money needed for use as capital funds commonly is supplied by "absentee owners." They contract to receive rewards solely if profit is earned and devoted in whole or in part to paying dividends. In any case some persons, usually known as owners, must supply the "equity" capital.

5. It is wholly natural that there will soon evolve the objective of trying to make money by striving to sell items of output for more money than the money disbursed as costs and expenses, when these latter have been properly allocated to the items sold.

Those who became merchants and concentrated on marketing during the several centuries prior to 1776 simply were striving to do what came naturally. Indeed, it is difficult and perhaps impossible for one to conjure up some different reasonable objective. Money-making as the controlling aim was originated unwittingly and evolved sans any prior planning. Those businessmen antedating 1776 ought not to have been roundly criticized and simply condemned. Smith, the Professor of Moral Philosophy, did condemn them and aimed for eradication of the money-making they were pursuing. Instead, he should have worked scientifically to analyze and understand the clear reality.

When one has acquired an adequate understanding of the financial institutions *naturally*, actually *wittingly,* evolved by merchants, ship owners, and artificers during the five centuries prior to Adam Smith, and of the functioning of those financial institutions, he will see that the incomes created for potential buyers of end-products fall distinctly short of equaling the aggregate of prices demanded by sellers. "Supply-side" economists are equally as mistaken as are "demand side" economists (and all other recognized schools of economists) in their theorizing about how highly developed free enterprise works.

In summary, the free enterprise system without piling up (in prosperity) more and more debts *might* be made to function and to survive in a marginally satisfactory way IF nearly all production, the marketing as well as the making, were by very small ventures in which the owners who supply all capital funds were also always managers and/or workers whose salaries and/or wages would reward them sufficiently to keep them in business and functioning on the average; then Say's Law *might* be forced to apply. But the reality is that great economies of scale have caused a tiny number of the countable ventures to grow to such huge size (with overwhelming aggregate financial volume) that each necessarily has raised great sums of equity capital funds from absentee owners so that, in order to be successful and to reward those equity owners out of "profits earned," it is required that sales revenues exceed the cost and expense payments that have been incurred. Both corporate law and corporate accounting require that there first be earnings out of which dividends properly may be distributed. Hence Say's Law fails to apply to or describe this factual reality. Contrary to the main assumption in that so-called "law," the cost and expense payments incurred by big firms are not sufficient to create incomes for potential buyers of end-products that equal the prices put on their output, the money profits sought being what that shortfall of incomes naturally turns out to be. Analysts must face the realities of corporate accounting and corporate law as well as the actual way in which money payments move counter to the time-consuming step-by-step production of output.

APPENDIX TO CHAPTER 3

This appendix is aimed to help readers who are trying to evaluate this work objectively to avoid being roadblocked by a quite specious allegation likely championed by adherents to diverse orthodox economics theory systems. It is usual for persons regarded as leaders in any field of knowledge to strive determinedly to maintain notions to which they have made commitments, even long after better ideas have been offered. Witness the reaction among his peers of the view by Columbus that the world is a sphere. Similarly many economists will surely advance the contention that the compilation of national income (symbolized commonly as "Y") and national product (symbolized as "G.N.P.") figures show that the total of the two are equal after some logical adjustments are made. Those adjustments are not being challenged here. It is the general idea of equivalence between aggregate incomes generated and the value of output that is being denied and charged with being quite false. Indeed, if the statistics on G.N.P. and Y prove anything they show on adequate cogitation that business payments of costs and expenses in the creation of incomes for potential buyers of output leave a marked gap that is filled otherwise, by supplementary means. This is demonstrated by the fact that in order to reach an equivalence between the value of aggregate product and total incomes in the computation there is included the important item of "corporate profits." Without the inclusion of corporate profits, Y would be very markedly less than the G.N.P. (not referring to or considering the "adjustments," which here are not challenged). Yet, as mentioned earlier and explained more fully later, corporate profits do put in their appearance mainly because of the absorption into business accounts of the effects of certain artificial financial expansions. Devoid of the effects of such artificial financial expansions that become melded into accounting records, national income would fall far short of equaling the "value" of the product. As an illustration, somewhat in anticipation of later detailed descriptions, in the year between mid-1984 and mid-1985, the outstanding consumer installment debt in the U.S. expanded by more than 20% or close to $100 billion. It was an increase from almost $400 billion in mid-1984 to almost $500 billion in mid-1985. While a part of that expansion represents the spending of borrowed savings, especially as thrift institutions have been getting into the act, much of the extension of installment credit in recent decades has involved the creation of new money by commercial banks lending to installment buyers directly or indirectly via finance companies. Hence in that year, it is a good guess, a guess because such lending often is so indirect through intermediaries that precise figures are impossible, that commercial banks supplied consumer buyers many billions of newly created dollars, possibly $50 billion. Consumers used this money to supplement their incomes in making purchases, mostly of "big ticket items" and credit card purchases. Consumers apparently spent a lot more money than their incomes supplied. Corporate sellers obviously were enabled to sell at prices averaging more than their costs and expenses of production. Moreover, there is considerable reason to believe that the artificial expansions of financial elements, such as the added money supply newly created by commercial banking, may generate business profits in ratio much greater than merely one-to-one, possibly some multiple, such as 2, 3, or 4-to-1. If much of the item of corporate profits is removed from Y, then the statistics help to prove that Y and G.N.P. would not come out equal in the compilations if money incomes were confined to those generated by businesses meeting costs and expenses.

CHAPTER 4

Mercantilism— I
In Antiquity, Particularly
in Western Civilization
The Natural Development
of Money-Making

The word "Mercantilism," which good dictionaries define as having the same meaning as "mercantile system" and sometimes as "commercial system," seems to have been employed by historians only within the last few decades. Adam Smith used "mercantile system" to describe the profits-pursuing or money-making objective and methods that the great merchants of his day, particularly those carrying on international trade, had evolved to a high state of importance in Great Britain during the three or four centuries prior to publication of his . . . *Wealth of Nations*. "Mercantilism" is adopted for use here because it is shorter and entirely sufficient.

The reader is cautioned that in this chapter "mercantilism" is applied to the same basic goal and processes the merchants and ship owners evolved in Western Europe in the early modern period, but to a very different time period. The controlling objective of those early modern traders came altogether naturally to be that of making money. Likewise, it turns out that since commerce in antiquity in Western civilization led international traders, ship owners, and even bill-of-exchange bankers to evolve that same financial objective, those operations in ancient times also can be described as "mercantilism."

Large-scale commerce in that earlier period did gave birth to the same financial objective. That is attested to by the fact that the Greeks had a word for it, namely, "chrematistics." It has been reported that this word was used in the writings of Aristotle.

Just a modest amount of cogitation will lead one to see that there is no basis for being surprised that leading traders in our ancient western civilization also developed the same money-making objective as the large-scale traders some hundreds of years later. Such is and was natural almost as soon as any thoroughgoing division of labor had arisen. Such division of labor most easily takes place first as a splitting off of marketing functions, the creation of place and time and ownership utilities, with some persons or families concentrating their attention on commerce. Any such developments do require and did require money to be raised for use as capital funds from which payments can be made for costs (for capital goods and for stock-in-trade) and expenses (for payment of employee wages and to buy provisions and to pay tolls and possibly for transport and even for the lodging of caravan members). Thus money circulates when payments are made from capital funds. In time, the velocity of its income circulation is the same rate as production flows in the opposite direction. Finally, those who have become merchants sell their merchandise inventory to acquire money again. It is simply natural that each such functionary will judge his venture to be a success or a failure in terms of the amount of money he recovers via his sales. If in the end he has obtained more money on the average than the costs and expenses incurred, the venture can be appraised as having been successful. The objective has evolved to being that of making money.

Indeed it is difficult to conjure up any alternative objective, other than that of making money. It need be not in the least surprising that large-scale marketing venturers in the ancient world, especially around the Mediterranean Sea, evolved without fail the controlling objective of making money. Only those traders who remained so small that they did not try to distinguish their business costs and expenses from their household expenses (as a huge number of small farmers and other very small ventures here in the U.S. commonly have not) could they very easily avoid striving to make money.

At this juncture there now is issued a request for help. Because of this author's too meager knowledge of the details of ancient history, of Western civilization as well as that of the Middle East and the Far East, he seeks aid in discovering whether or not the traders among our ancestors in antiquity in Europe developed any special methods to help assure success of their ventures, especially in the macro-chrematistics sense. The Mercantilists in the first centuries of the modern era (from about 1300 until about the 1720s) developed and pressed vigorously to have certain methods, including much regulation, adopted and instituted by sovereign authority. They did this to help assure that they could make money on the whole. Since the 1720s, the Modern Mercantilists, spread to many other lines in addition to marketing, with an importance many times that of commerce, have come to rely on a quite different financial technique for assuring overall success in the macro-chrematistics sense. Was there any particular method or methods devised by traders in ancient times to help make sure that collectively they could attain financial success?

Further questions well up and beg in one's mind for help in

rounding out our insights. Civilizations in the Far East (Eastern Asia) go back even further than do those more direct ancestors of the U.S. For example, to what extent did the trade that developed in antiquity in various parts of Asia also evolve that same money-making objective? Since the pursuit of money profits tends to develop so naturally and is so easily grasped, any alternative objective would be somewhat awkward to devise. What did happen along these lines in those early Eastern civilizations?

Wherever there has been adherence to essentially free enter-prise in diverse areas anywhere during the last two millenniums, has the pursuit of money profits also evolved as soon as significant division of labor began to be prominent? Have special methods been devised or advocated to assure success in money-making in the overall or macro-chrematistics sense?

CHAPTER 5

Mercantilism— II
From the Crusades
to 1720

Money-Making that Relied on
Favorable Trade Balances

According to many commentators, "Mercantilism," called by many writers including Adam Smith "The Mercantile System," usually is regarded as having existed in Western Europe from about 1500, or a bit earlier, until about 1800. There is a great overlap of that period and the slightly more than four centuries in the period covered in this chapter. The purpose of going back further than most writers in tracing mercantilism is to include mention of its origin and the natural development of profits-seeking business, and to tie in the connection with the evolution of the special techniques that were devised to help assure that such free enterprise business firms could be successful, in the collective or macro-chrematistics sense, in realizing their principal and controlling objective. Mercantilism was not eradicated around 1720 nor around 1800 despite Adam Smith's criticism of it and recommendations against it. On the contrary it has grown even more vigorously since 1720, from which juncture it began to spread rapidly into many phases of activity besides trade and commerce. By now producing business firms pursuing that same money-making objective have become overwhelmingly dominant. Beginning around 1720 such businesses have come to rely on a new and very different principal process or method or technique to help them apparently succeed in the collective or macro-chrematistics sense. Accordingly, it seems useful to discuss mercantilism in the modern period in two distinct parts: in this chapter, prior to around 1720, and in the next chapter, from the 1720s until the present time.

Part 1. The Wholly Natural Origin and Evolution of Absentee-Owned Capitalism With Its Controlling Goal o f Making Money Profits

Emphasis in this section is placed upon the word "natural" and the "naturalness" of the mercantilistic system which evolved and grew ever more important as the result of the division of labor. Indeed it seems difficult to conceive of any alternative evolution at all logical in a really free enterprise system.

It has been remarked earlier that true division of labor, not mere specialization of members of a household or even between households, first arises when persons begin to concentrate their attention and efforts on marketing. Split-off marketing creates time, place, and ownership utilities for products "made" by several other households creating form utility, whether by handicraft or by agriculture or even by hunting and fishing.

Some of the traders from Western Europe in the very early

modern period tended to use overland routes to Asia Minor, routes that sometimes had been used by Crusaders. Their purpose was to buy and bring home some of those exotic items they had experienced while trying to redeem the Holy Land. Sea routes were sometimes used. However, the Crusades, involving large numbers of men with weapons and armor and horses, had found land travel more suitable.

Of course one who ventured to be a trader, especially to carry on commerce across several sovereign principalities, did not go alone. He might join with others who independently were undertaking similar ventures. Or he might contract with others to undertake a joint venture. He might, if he could raise sufficient money capital, organize a caravan of his own by buying or leasing the transport equipment and animals needed and hiring employees to supply the hands required. In any case a sole undertaker would have to meet money costs of equipment and supplies and money expenses for wages, for lodging, for sustenance, and often for tolls, et cetera. If some or most of the movement were by water, many of the expenses would be somewhat different than if by land; however, the need for money capital funds and disbursement of money payments out of such capital funds would be essentially similar.

After a period of time, if nothing went awry with the project, the merchant would have returned to his base in the west and would have goods to sell. Of course he would need to sell his stock-in-trade for money, at least sufficient money to recoup that money which was paid out to meet the costs and expenses he had incurred.

In time traders in Western Europe, particularly those from England, came to deal more and more in goods that moved both ways. They would take eastward woolens and their derivative products and bring west exotic items, including spices and perfumes and silks, items of relatively high value. Eventually the processing of wool evolved into the "putting out" or "cottage" system. This system was devised by English merchants of rising wealth and importance whose agents used the technique of supplying muscle-driven spinning, or weaving, or carding equipment on the one hand and the raw material or partly finished goods on the other hand to families scattered in cottages in the rural areas. When the members of a household had completed the processing assigned to them, an agent of the merchant came and paid for the work done and carried away the semi-finished or finished output. Obviously, the putting-out or cottage system required the merchant involved to raise still greater amounts of money for use as capital funds and incur cost and expense payments even earlier. Clearly, the money used began to take on a circular flow or income circulation movement with a velocity comparable to the rate of the flow of products through their making and marketing steps. What would any merchant thus engaged naturally set as his main or first objective? The making of some money profit, of course. Further suppose that the venture grew to be relatively large, having several partners or even became a chartered company with several equity owners. What basic objective would they or could they set for their firm except that of making money?

Is it not simply the nature of the situation, as soon as men begin to concentrate their efforts on marketing, the obvious first step in true division of labor, to accumulate money to use as capital funds, some of which must be employed to cover the costs and expenses necessarily incurred, and then finally have stock-in-trade goods to sell, that they try vigorously to sell those items for more money than they have paid out of those capital funds?

Incidentally, the Roman Catholic Church may be credited with a minor amount of responsibility for making inevitable the pursuit of money-profits. During the many centuries of the Middle Ages, that Church was the one powerful unifying force in most of Western Europe. In that area during many hundreds of years, the most common need for borrowed funds was to aid individuals and families who had fallen upon hard times and were experiencing some sort of trouble. It was a very rare need to borrow for business use and since it would be unchristian for lenders to reap benefits from the misfortune of others, the Church disapproved of interest-taking. Hence later, when friends, relatives, or even persons simply seeking possible rewards helped to furnish money capital funds for a trading venture, they usually would be partners, active participants, or simply owners of some sort of the equity. Absentee-owners were almost inevitable in any considerable enterprise, in part because of the prohibition of interest-taking decreed by the Church. How then could such owners be rewarded? The almost inescapable answer is by being paid profits-rewards in terms of more money than originally supplied as capital. This was sooner or later, by one means or another, expected to be returned to them. How else?

Let one ponder the coming of double-entry accounting. W.C. Mitchell in his *Business Cycles: The Problem and Its Setting* asserted that double-entry accounting was "invented" in Italy in 1494. However, "invented" is scarcely the correct word. For what was done was merely to formalize, to put into logical order, that which the leading merchants had in fact been doing for a very long time, even if with less satisfactory record-keeping. Two elements of double-entry accounting deserve special attention in this presentation. First, such accounting regards the business enterprise as a separate entity, apart from the individual (or individuals) who supply the equity capital funds. The latter persons are treated simply as residual obligees who are entitled to all that is left after creditors and others having valid claims against the business are properly satisfied. Second, double-entry accounting through its whole life has sanctioned the distribution of dividends (apart from "liquidating dividends") only out of profits or earnings that previously have been "made" and recorded.

This suggests that it is worthwhile to mention the rise of business corporations, the first of which began to appear many centuries past. Such a corporation, created by sovereign authority usually on request of several persons desiring to engage in a joint venture, was decreed to be a separate legal entity apart from equity owners. It, too, simply put into a more workable form what some individuals and partnerships were evolving. It fitted hand-in-glove with double-entry accounting as well as the idea that any dividend (not a "liquidating dividend") is to be disbursed only out of profits already recorded as earned through having made sales at prices which exceed the costs and expenses properly allocated to the items sold. Indeed, corporate law naturally included, from its beginning, denial of any right to distribute any dividends (except "liquidating dividends") out of capital funds. That meaning seems clear.

Part 2. The Transcendent Efforts to Realize Favorable Balances of Trade.

As one studies the writings descriptive of mercantilism between the Crusades and the present time, those prior to 1720 as well as since, he will recognize that all commentators emphasize the need of the mercantilists in each leading trading nation in Western Europe to realize continuously a favorable balance of trade. The obvious purpose was to maintain an inflow of money from abroad. If one considers only recent writers, it is possible he will get the impression that the principal purpose of striving to realize such a favorable balance was to strengthen the "home" nation to the highest possible extent. That interpretation does place the emphasis in the wrong place. The great merchants in the leading trading nations did desire a strong and unified nation of considerable size. However, their initial and main purpose was to assure that they could sell for a money profit, and could make money in the macro-chrematistics sense. Even as one reads carefully Smith's . . . *Wealth of Nations* he will see that the underlying drive of the merchants for an inflow of money metals was their trying forever to "turn a penny where a penny is to be got."

The merchants in Western Europe in the first few centuries of the modern era did foster and champion a central sovereign and a strong national government. They did this at first to break down provincial barriers and to afford protection to caravans and to shipping, then a bit later to conquer available, more backward, peoples. They concentrated on appropriating accumulated precious metals as spoils of war, and establishing colonies sometimes of native peoples and sometimes by sending colonists from the mother country. They regulated the colonial inhabitants so as to induce those to supply cheaply raw materials and products needed by the empire's home processors. They regulated and kept low the wages of the workers at home so as to hold down the costs of products destined for export. All of these actions and regulations were intended to help bring into some one of those leading business nations of Western Europe, more and more, ever more, precious metals that were used as money. Obviously if the big traders were able nearly continuously to realize a favorable balance of trade (more accurately, but virtually identical "favorable balance of payments") they would be able to sell their stock-in-trade for more money than had been their money costs and expenses. They would be able to make money and to prosper in the macro-chrematistics sense. Also if a nation's central government were able through conquest to obtain important accumulations of precious metals as spoils of war, such money metals likely in a reasonable lapse of time would be put into circulation, as by paying soldiers and sailors and other expenses. Thus, it would be used to increase the spending power of buyers of end-products beyond the money incomes created for them by the payments (including some taxes) made by merchant-businessmen as these latter incurred costs and expenses.

It is to be presumed that with the rise again of long-distance trading in the early modern era, merchants being few and their ventures relatively small, even if those few did succeed on the whole in garnering more money as they made their sales than the money they had paid to meet their costs and expenses, the effect was virtually unnoticeable. However, as the collective volume of business of the merchants grew and grew and grew through the centuries following the Crusades, their coming to possess a growing portion of a nation's precious-metal money (while little or none of such metals was being produced in Western Europe) surely the effects began to be felt — and regarded by some citizens, such as Smith, as an evil. Clearly with the passage of a few centuries following the rebirth in the long-distance trading, an urgent need for somehow acquiring more money for circulation began to seem very pressing. It was not unnatural nor unexpected that in time some diverse leaders of that period thought up the favorable balance of trade (or payments) method as the means of overcoming the perceived difficulty. As always, with business there seemed to be a shortage of and need for more money. And any nation, in the sense of the government authority and organization, would prosper too, when and if much additional acceptable money could be imported. Finally, it seemed that any nation's people prospered along with the merchants and the central government.

Incidentally, it is worth remarking that a "colonial" area that was backward in the technology of making and manufacturing things might find or extract considerable quantities of those metals used as standard money. This was true of certain lands in the New World. When its people could trade newly acquired money metals for manufactures from Western Europe, especially if those goods came in at reasonable prices with a modest markup for profit, the citizens at both ends of the deal were benefited.

CHAPTER 6

Mercantilism— III:
From the 1720s to the 1980s

The Spread of the Money-Making Objective to Engulf Most Production of Form Utilities and Its Growth to Overwhelming Dominance.

The Concurrent Rise of Money-Creating Banking Which Has Supplied the Money-Making Pursuit a Powerful New Method

Part 1-A. The Great Branching Out of the Money-Making Objective to Big Producing Firms Other Than Those Engaged in Commerce

It has been observed from time to time earlier that true and significant division of labor first appeared when some individuals or households began to devote their main, if not their full, attention and efforts to marketing products which other individuals or household had "made," commonly along with producing much for their own consumption. Such "making" usually was devoid of involving any money costs. Merchants and ship captains and any others who devoted themselves to the creation solely of time, and/or place, and/or ownership utilities really were the first capitalists. They found it necessary to raise money somehow to use as capital funds to pay the costs and expenses they incurred in carrying on their businesses. They continued, until into the early 1700s, to be nearly alone — those capitalists who naturally evolved and embraced the profits, or money-making, pursuit.

However, things began to take on a faster pace and broadened out into much wider activities as a result of the "putting out" system that had become the surviving method of turning out textiles, particularly woolens, in England and Great Britain. The simplified and frequently repeated motions required of humans led, not unnaturally, to the conjuring up of some mechanical arms which could make one or more of those same motions and could do so unerringly at a faster and faster pace. Almost concurrently the steam engine was devised and improved until by 1760 it had been "perfected" by James Watt and became available to drive the then-appearing motion-making textile machines. The engine supplemented the water power already in use. It is not surprising that economic historians date the Industrial Revolution, a struggle between old and new techniques of making or manufacturing, first textiles and later more and more other items, between 1760 and 1840. By the latter date the new factory system had won dominance and earlier methods had been proved passe'. In many lines of making goods, especially those in which numerous distinct motions were involved in turning out a finished item, each motion could be made by a machine using inanimate power. By the middle of the 1800s, especially in Britain, the factory system was firmly established.

The Great Inventions, in textiles using steam power, were

followed soon by the application of the steam engine to powering locomotives and ships. Hence railroads were developed and provided much improved and less costly land transport along with improved and cheaper water carriage. Later the steam engine made possible the construction of electric generators and served to power them. Hence "inanimate power" became, with improved electricity generation and transmission and distribution, far more flexible because it was easily turned on and off as well as transportable everywhere. Electricity generation and transmission and distribution further led to the development of the electric light bulb which made many activities, including factory operations, fully possible during nighttime hours as well as during daylight hours. A bit later came the invention of the internal combustion engine, making use of the power in liquid fossil fuel ignited by an electric spark in a closed chamber. That was made to drive a piston connected to a rod which was fastened to a crankshaft which converted a back-and-forth (or up-and-down) motion into a rotary motion. The automobile, truck, and the airplane followed. A close cousin of the gasoline internal-combustion engine (if not its descendant) is the diesel engine. This engine makes only a small use of the electric spark to start, and has come to be used mainly in work-horse occupations, such as in trucks, locomotives, power generators, some ships, and even, with adaptation, in jet airplanes. Indeed since the fore part of the 1900s gasoline and diesel engines are used more and more in agriculture, displacing some few earlier steam engines. Following another line, the harnessing of electricity has made possible the development of the telegraph, the telephone, the radio, television, and ultimately the computer and many kindred items.

The purpose of listing the inventions and development of machines that help create "form utilities," once the Great Inventions began to be introduced in the first half of the 1700s, is to recall the mammoth advances made these last two and one-half centuries in the division of labor and to explain the widespread need for large firms and large assemblages of money capital funds. Before the 1720s, big enterprises were confined in the main to those ventures engaged in marketing or commerce. By the ninth decade of the twentieth century here in the U.S., those many business firms concentrating on factory manufacturing, on communication and broadcasting, on transportation, or on extraction, exceed both in financial size and in number of employees those enterprises engaged in handling goods, creating one or a combination of marketing utilities. In each of several lines of creating utilities a venture must be relatively quite large in order to take full advantage of the benefits of division of labor and to realize the maximum economies of scale. Therefore each such firm, required to be big in order to excel in competition, must raise large sums of money for use as capital funds. Each firm must disburse money in order to meet money costs and expenses of production, and thus it participates in helping to create money incomes for potential buyers via the circuit flow with a circuit velocity matching that of the flow of output. Naturally it strives in the end to recover through its sales more money than its costs and expenses. Thus it hopes to realize net earnings (or profits) out of which it can distribute profits-rewards to its absentee owners. That same principle, actually the controlling objective evolved naturally by the earlier mercantilists, continues in full command these last two hundred fifty years. However, it now is more pervasive and dominant both in economic and chrematistic activities.

Part 1-B. The Overwhelming Importance of Big Producing Firms, U.S., 1970s and 1980s

It has been asserted that when an enterprise must become very large in order to develop the full potential of division of labor and of the economies of scale, much money capital usually is required, various portions of which must be paid out to meet costs and expenses of producing. These money disbursements in turn circulate at the same velocity as production flows and thus create incomes for potential buyers of end-products. The prices realized by the producer-sellers in disposing of their output must exceed the money they have paid out if they are to garner enough so that absentee-owners, who supplied the initial funds, can be rewarded through profits distributions.

However, those steps often are not necessary for very small firms since the owner (or partners) may not need to be rewarded through profits earned. For them, other compensation, such as wages or salaries, is often sufficient to keep them functioning. Indeed many very minute ventures may be scarcely more than operating as self-sufficient households. Commonly they do not distinguish between their "business" disbursements and their household expenses. However the relatively few big firms have grown so huge on the average that they exceed by many times the combined output of the far more numerous small ventures.

Ponder the statistical information published by *Fortune* in its issue of April 29, 1985, pp. 266-284. It lists what it has found to be the 500 largest industrial firms in the U.S. in 1984.

Those 500 largest industrial firms in the U.S. in 1984 collectively had $1,758,721,251,000 of sales, (i.e., $1 & 3/4 trillion, initial letter is "T")

$1,409,565,773,000 of assets ($1.4 trillion, initial letter is "T")

$86,402,025,000 of net income (more than $86 billion, initial letter is "B")

$636,932,682,000 of stockholder equity (about $637 billion, initial letter is "B")

14,195,792 employees (more than 14 million, initial letter is "M")

At this juncture special attention is called only to the last figure above. Those 500 of this nation's largest industrial firms employed approximately one-seventh (1/7) of the whole of our workers then holding jobs.

The June 10, 1985, issue of *Fortune*, pp. 175-195, presents another list of 500 of the largest firms in the U.S. in 1984, this time in seven categories of non-industrial companies. They are classified into (1) 100 Diversified Service Co., (2) 100 Commercial Banking Co., (3) 100 Diversified Financial Co., (4), 50 Life Insurance Co., (5) 50 Retailing Co., (6) 50 Transportation Co., and (7) 50 Utilities. It might be doubted that some of these mentioned firms are in the main "producing" while, on the other hand, the data for life insurance companies in some respects is not comparable to figures for other categories of firms, since half of those insurance companies are mutuals. Accordingly, in the summary that follows, consideration of the 100 largest Commercial Banking companies and of the 100 largest diversified financial companies and the 50 largest life insurance companies is omitted.

As one gives attention only to the largest 100 diversified service companies and 50 each of retailing companies and of transportation companies and of utilities, all of which indubitably seem to be producer firms as production is defined by economists, he obtains from the *Fortune* data the following numbers for 1984:

The sum of their sales (or revenue) was $814,261,514,000 ($814.3 "B"illion)

The sum of their assets was $934,092,955,000 ($914.1 "B"illion)

The sum of their net incomes was $42,126,766,000 ($42.1 "B"illion)

The sum of their stockholders' equity was $311,278,365,000 ($311.3 "B"illion)

The sum of their employees was 7,474,089 (7.5 "M"illion)

Let the data for those 750 individual firms, 500 largest industrials plus 100 largest diversified service plus 50 each largest retailers and transportation and utility companies be added all together. That 750 U.S. firms collectively had in 1984:

Total sales (or revenue) of $2,572,982,365,000 (almost $2.6 "T"rillion)

Total assets of $2,343,458,728,000 (many billions more than $2.3 "T"rillion)

Total net incomes of $128,528,791,000 (millions more than $128.5 "B"illion)

Total stockholders' equity of $948,211,047,000 (a bit more than $948.2 "B"illion)

Total employee summing to 21,669,881 (several thousand less than 21.7 "M"illion)

Note again that these huge figures are those combined for only the 750 largest, 500 industrial and 250 non-industrial, firms engaged largely in producing. The number of these separate entities is only as many as can be counted on the fingers and toes of 37 homo sapiens who have completely normal limbs plus 1 double-amputee. These very few large firms in 1984 employed right at one-fifth (20%) of the workers in the nation who then had jobs. Probably almost none of those employees were working part-time. Likely it is correct to conclude that those 750 largest firms engaged in producing in the U.S. in 1984 were corporations. All firms were using great sums of money as capital funds. All firms were paying out from such funds money to meet costs and expenses of their producing activities. These money disbursements were circulating against the flow of goods, quid pro quo, with the same circuit velocity. All firms were striving like the earlier mercantilists to make money in the end by attempting to realize or garner selling prices in excess of costs and expenses per the principles of double-entry accounting and the legal prohibition against any corporation making distribution from capital funds in the guise of earnings.

Now consider some data that portray an overall picture of the business financial community, of which the few huge firms are in terms of numbers of entities a very minute part. The figures that follow are not to be compared directly with those already set forth, since they apply to entrepreneurships in 1977 in the U.S. The following numbers are taken from the 1981 *Statistical Abstract of the U.S.* and, as always, are several years "late," since they are compiled in intermittent years from the federal tax returns. While not current, 1977 was about as "normal" a year as any recent one. The proportions that will be emphasized continue about the same even though the absolute counts likely have increased a bit with the passage of seven years.

According to the 1981 *Statistical Abstract*, in 1977 there were in the U.S. 14,741,000 (a little under 15 "M"illion) "businesses" and collectively they realized sales or revenues that totaled $4,384,300,000,000 (about $4 & 3/8 "T"rillion). However, only 358,000 of those firms (about 2.4% of the total) each enjoyed revenues in 1977 of $1,000,000 or more. Collectively that small number took in a total of $3,594,100,000,000 (almost $3.6 "T"rillion). Hence those few "big firms" had average receipts of almost $10,000,000. By contrast the remaining 14,383,000 (14.4 - "M"illion) "little" firms (97.6% of the entrepreneurships) averaged a bit less than $55,000 revenue each in 1977. The sales or receipts of the "big" firms came to fully 82% of those realized by the whole 14,741,000. Further, 314,000 of the "big" enterprises were corporations while only 41,000 of the ventures that garnered receipts of $1,000,000 were not corporations. Those "big" corporations enjoyed in 1977 average net earnings of $717,000. The net earnings for "big" sole proprietorships and partnerships cannot be set forth, since they are not reported or published separately. The "little" enterprises plus all of the 41,000 "big" sole proprietorships and partnerships realized total net incomes collectively of $89,300,000,000 (just under $90 "B"illion). Hence they had average net incomes of only $6,100 in 1977. The total net earnings of the 314,000 corporations that took in $1 million or more in revenue came to 71.6% of the total net profit recorded by the whole of the almost 15 million "business" firms in 1977. With the 41,000 "million-dollar" non-corporate businesses added to the "million dollar" corporations, the whole 358,000 garnered at least 75% of earnings available for equity owners — and probably employed at least 75% of the workers who had jobs at that time.

The 1977 statistical data permit clarification and evaluation of one of the highly intriguing lines of reasoning in economic theory, namely with respect to "normal price" (which latter is asserted to include "a minimum necessary profit" because if producers fail to realize that much on the average, they will cease) toward which "market price" is supposed to be driven by competition. That might be fairly valid about the vast majority of little entrepreneurships, say fully 14,000,000 little firms in the U.S. in 1977 out of the 14,741,000 total of all enterprises. Remember that 14,383,000 of them that year had average sales (or revenues) of only about $55,000 and average net income of only $6,100. Accordingly, fully 95% of all U.S. business ventures in 1977 must have been relatively quite small, overwhelmingly proprietorships and partnerships in which the owner or owners were participating as managers or as workers. Often they had little or no capital funds at risk. Also, very often they did not really distinguish between business costs and expenses on the one hand and household or family expenses on the other. They did not need to do so if not a corporation. Indeed they simply were functioning as small farmers, "mom and pop" retail stores, neighborhood bakeries, flower shops, auto repair garages, restaurants and real estate agents, et cetera. Most of them always have functioned simply to "get a living" rather than "to make money" (although some do). In contrast, if taking full advantage of the potential for division of labor and the economies of scale means that the enterprise must become very large and assemble huge collections of capital funds, the surviving competitors necessarily shrink to but a few, and are each organized as a separate entity with absentee owners of the final equity. Accordingly every one of the survivors in such a producing situation will find it both natural and necessary to pursue money-making.

The treatment through the whole of this analysis really concerns that small fraction, say 2.4%, of all enterprises which does 75% or more of the total production volume of the nation. It necessarily becomes a chrematistics analysis. Further, it leaves on the opposing side of the coin, say 97.6% of the ventures, those small "participatory entrepreneurships" that are not necessarily run on the need for making money. The very minute number of very large firms dominates. Separate and careful attention must be focused on analyzing them and their financial system. In terms of their controlling objective, they are twentieth-century Mercantilists.

Part 2. The Origin, Development, and Reliance on Money-Creating Banking.

By the 1720s the big producing firms that had come to pursue money-making as their first and controlling objective were influenced in a major way by the coming of the kind of banking that creates added money which normally is inserted and added to the nation's medium of exchange. Such money-creating banks historically have been known as "commercial banks." In the last twenty years or so some "thrift institutions" have adopted those methods, too, but usually to only a very limited extent. The creation of added new money by private individuals and firms was a wholly unplanned and unwitting development. Even today it appears that numerous well-versed citizens, including many who can be called "bankers," do not believe that it can be or is being done. There was a lapse of approximately two centuries from the very beginning of the process until it was completely understood.

Money-creating banking was sparked by the simple arrangement, wholly innocent of any such intention, of several people or firms in possession of considerable cash contracting to employ others to hold such funds for safekeeping. Other kinds of operations called "banking" preceded, some by many centuries, the origin of money-creating banking. These included money-changing banks to exchange one area's medium for that of another, banks to exchange full-bodied coins for others that were deteriorated, and bills-of-exchange banks that permitted offsetting payments at a distance, payments that needed to be made in opposite directions by different people. The latter was done so that the money from payers at each end was actually used to pay those close by who had money coming from the other end of that considerable distance. Money-creating banking was started, unwittingly and completely unplanned, from a much simpler process — that of leaving (or depositing) money for safekeeping.

This began in London from the unlikely spark set off by "The Forced Loan of 1640." Several leading merchants in London by the early 1600s had grown rich enough and possessed of enough "coin of the realm" that they were concerned to arrange for the money's safekeeping when their business establishments were closed. Over time they came to use for that purpose the Tower of London, which was guarded through twenty-four hours every day by the King's soldiers. All seemed to go well until in 1640 the King, finding himself in serious need of more funds, on his initiative alone "borrowed" the money that the merchants had deposited there. That started actions that brought on privately owned, money-creating "commercial banking." Almost at once after that 1640 forced loan, those London merchants, wanting a more secure depository, began to employ goldsmiths, who were concentrated in the vicinity of Lombard Street, for that purpose, since a goldsmith naturally provided himself with a strongbox and one or more watchmen commonly during non-business hours. He advantageously could earn a bit more income if he were to receive and hold on deposit the funds of one or several of the rich merchants, especially when their establishments were closed.

If one were a merchant who took his money to his goldsmith for overnight deposit, he, of course, would require and obtain either a receipt or something of the nature of a "pass-book." The book would likely show deposits on one side (or column) and withdrawals on the other side (or column). Obviously if the merchant, or his agent, reclaimed the whole of the money deposited on the next business day he would surrender all receipts or, instead, the withdrawal entries in his passbook would be recorded as precisely offsetting and balancing the deposits. Each merchant could receive back the identical money units he had deposited. So far, so good.

Another factor soon entered the picture — the principle of "the conservation of energy" or "human laziness." All that was required to turn those goldsmiths into bankers was for merchants to leave deposits of money in the possession of their respective goldsmiths during their business hours as well as when their businesses were closed. They could do this even as the money deposits were being used to make payments. A depositor could sign over one (or more) goldsmith's receipt and deliver it to a payee with instruction to go get the funds, arrangements having been made by such depositor for the goldsmith to honor his endorsement. If a passbook were used (instead of receipts), arrangements could have been made with the depositor's goldsmith to honor his correctly drawn and signed "negotiable-order-of-withdrawal" to a payee who would identify himself properly to the goldsmith. A crucial thing to note is that often the payee, who brought to a goldsmith an endorsed receipt issued by the latter or a "negotiable-order-of-withdrawal" (a "check") against a valid deposit, would be already a depositor with the same goldsmith. In this case, the title to the specified amount of money simply would be shifted from one depositor (payor) to another (payee), while the actual coin-of-the-realm remained untouched, apparently lying idle. However, if the payee-recipient of an endorsed receipt or of a valid negotiable-order-of-withdrawal on one goldsmith possessed a deposit with a different goldsmith, it nearly at once was found to be easier and simpler for him to take it directly to his own goldsmith and make a deposit. This goldsmith would be instructed to obtain the actual money from the first. Almost as quickly as this short-circuited process began to be used, it was discovered that while the second goldsmith was receiving for deposit one or more claims against the first goldsmith, transactions in the opposite direction were occurring, too. Claims received by one goldsmith were approximately matched and offset by similar claims in the opposite direction. In effect, in "clearing" the ostensible money movements in the two directions, those two goldsmiths in the main simply began to trade their claims against each other. Of course a bit of a difference often might remain to be settled in cash in one direction or the other. However, since the "clearings" on all goldsmiths, considered collectively, would just about match and offset, very little coin-of-the-realm would require to be moved.

Of course the deposits held by goldsmiths had to be regarded, as they soon were, as "fungible" in the eyes of the law.

So the lawful money on deposit with a goldsmith naturally was observed to be apparently "lying idle" (even though title was being transferred from depositor to depositor). Since it was fungible, it belonged to the goldsmith. In time some goldsmiths would, of course, conjecture as to whether or not some of the idle money might be lent out at interest. One may be sure that certain potential borrowers, such as the King and members of the powerful royalty and nobility, on being apprised of the accumulation of idle coin, were eager to borrow. Some few loans began to be made, probably by goldsmiths with the least scruples.

However, the making of loans, ostensibly from goldsmith-held pools of idle coin-of-the-realm, did not result in such money moving out from their strongboxes. The borrower himself most likely would prefer to take the proceeds of his loan in the form of goldsmith receipts (perhaps several of them, each in a rounded denomination) or as a passbook deposit against which he could write negotiable-orders-of-withdrawal. So, the lawful money on deposit with any single goldsmith was apt to remain almost undiminished except that those who rushed ahead making loans faster and in larger volume than their peers were likely to encounter adverse clearings. The more liberal lenders lost money from their caches of coin, and the more conservative ones gained as much in the clearings processes. If lending by all goldsmiths were to go along at about the same rate and proportion, each would retain about the same amount of "vault money." Hence by moving about together those goldsmiths discovered that they could lend more and more and still more. They discovered, too, that it was not the lawful money held in their strongboxes that they were lending. That lawful money simply came to serve as their "reserves." They could lend two and three and four and five and even ten times as much so long as they felt able to meet the infrequent demand for lawful money. It was the goldsmith receipts (which evolved into bank notes) and the negotiable-orders-of-withdrawal against passbook deposits (which became checks against demand deposits) that were serving as money. These were circulating and serving to pay business costs and expenses, for products purchased, and to pay debts.

The goldsmiths and their progeny were creating added money by making more and more loans, the proceeds of which were taken as bank notes or as demand deposits circulated by checks through the clearings. By the 1720s this process had become well established and very powerful. Since then its influences and importance simply have multiplied further by many times.

With the birth and growth of money-creating banking, big producing firms that must and do strive to make money as their primary and controlling objective have come to use a new and more important process than before. That minor fraction of production carried on before the 1720s mainly by big merchant firms in order to make money had to rely mostly on bringing into their home country ever a little more and a little more additional money. This was done mostly by regulations designed to create favorable balances of trade. Since about the 1720s, when money-creating commercial banking really attained full power, the nations of Western Europe and eventually the U.S. found it possible to supply buyers increased money-purchasing power by making more and more commercial bank loans that enlarge the amount of money in circulation. It makes very little difference who does the borrowing and at what juncture in the circuit flow, since somewhere in that circle the purchasing power of potential buyers of end-products is augmented. Buyers can pay — as long as the volume of new loans being made exceeds the volume of old loans concurrently being paid — to big producer firms more money in acquiring the latter's output than those producers have incurred as money costs and expenses.

Of course enterprises striving to make money have not

forsaken altogether their earlier techniques. Often they continue to ask for tariffs and subsidies. However, primary reliance in the late twentieth century is on increases of the money supply by way of money-creating operations of our banks (not including our "thrift institutions" as long as they confine themselves to their historic types of service).

It seems to me that several postscripts may require to be added to the end of this chapter to forestall some readers, who might continue to believe that the conclusions described here are not correct, from grasping at straws, even fictitious straws, by denying and smugly dismissing from consideration what has been presented.

The first postscript concerns the source of present-day increases in the nation's circulating money supply. If one pays careful attention he will hear many commentators, even some who purport to be authorities, mention unjustifiably something about "the government printing money" or running the printing presses. The fact is that the actions of the U.S. federal government have almost nothing to do these last many decades with increases in the money supply. Those increases have come almost 100% from the operations of our banking system, including the monetary transactions of our Federal Reserve Banks which are owned in whole by the member banks. The sole way in which the central government increases a tiny bit the money in circulation is through the minting of fractional coins which are put into circulation in exchange for other money; as those new coins cost less for the material and the making than their money value, the mint makes money, a little profit.

One way to explain beyond doubt the manner in which our money supply has been enlarged during the last several decades is to consider the composition of what is included to compute "M1." This symbol is used most often to stand for the basic money supply. The following data are from Table 1.21 as set forth on

p. A13 of the September, 1985, issue of the *Federal Reserve Bulletin.*

Table 6-1
Money Stock, Liquid Assets and Debt Measures
Billions of dollars, average daily figures
Seasonally Adjusted

Item	Dec. 1983	Dec. 1984	June 1985
1 M1	528.0	558.5	591.2
M1 Components			
6 Currency	148.4	158.7	164.5
7 TravelersChecks	4.9	5.2	5.7
8 Demand Deposits	243.5	248.6	260.7
9 Other checkable deposits	131.3	146.0	160.3

The sole fraction of the M1 components actually put into circulation by "the government" are those fractional coins, and only as many of them will remain there as are required to facilitate making change. Even then they cost the government a good amount for the materials and the production expenses, so that net gain is but a small portion of what they sell for. In contrast the whole of our "folding money" outstanding now is issued, nearly always via member banks, by the Federal Reserve Banks. However, the Bureau of Engraving actually does print that paper money and supplies it unissued to the several Federal Reserve Agents. The F.R.Bs., in issuing those federal reserve notes, do so only as called for, and in exchange for other, proper financial or money instruments. By far the largest portion of the M1 growth is found in demand deposits (historically of "commercial banks") and other "checkable deposits" (mostly "NOW accounts" of "thrift institutions"). Those demand deposits and other checkable deposits generally rise as banking operations make a larger total of new loans than the loans concurrently being paid off. They shrink as more outstanding loans are being paid off and extinguished than the volume of new loans being made simultaneously. Incidentally, our commercial banks that are members of the Federal Reserve System are required to maintain relatively small reserves "behind" their demand deposits. Since the mid-1960s, those required reserves have been deposits to the credit of the respective member banks on the books of the F.R.B. of that district. The F.R.B. can increase the reserves of the member banks. The method most used to increase member bank reserves is the Federal Reserve System's buying up on the open market, without using any existing money of any sort, federal government debt obligations. This simply works to add the amount of the purchase price of those obligations to the deposit credit of member banks. Thus enlarging the member banks' reserves makes it possible for those banks legally to lend further several times more.

A second postscript may go far towards clarifying fully what has been said in the last half of this chapter, and also help anticipate and forestall a line of reasoning that many readers, especially bankers and a few business economists, might hope to believe in order to grasp as an acceptable alternative. One who is knowledgeable in economics and also in money and banking theory will have heard it asserted that if the commercial banks do create additional money, by making loans (new money which borrowers pay into circulation), that process usually or at least often helps to finance additional production so that more goods and services are turned out. Thus it is reasoned that there will be more goods forthcoming to absorb the money. Such loans of commercial bank credit often are made to appear beneficial by setting new lines of production in motion — that eventually will help to satisfy human wants more fully. When this line of thinking is asserted it seems possible for one to assume that everything has been said that deserves to be said. However there is a great shortcoming. More analysis is call for.

The basic portrayal here of the way new bank-created money, added to that already in circulation, can and does enable profits-pursuing, mercantilistic-type firms to record in their accounts sales at prices which exceed their properly allocated production costs and expenses, does not deny that such added money is often used to finance increased production. Those two aspects of the effects of inserting additional new bank-created money into use are not mutually exclusive and need not be in opposition. New "bank-money" can be used often both to help finance additional production and make possible recording of money profit in the chrematistics sense. For example, if one assumes that there exists unused manufacturing production facilities, such as plant and equipment and idle labor, a bank loan can supply money to buy labor and materials and power. However, on being used, some of that added money inevitably will be paid to potential consumers, such as workers, considerably prior to the arrival of the new output at the retail juncture. It will enable those consumers to spend more than the costs and expenses incurred by firms whose products are bought by them — items already available at retail. If the newly created money resulting from commercial bank operations is used to finance new plant and equipment, some of that added money, indeed much of it, will reach the retail level long before any additional output from such "being-built" capital equipment will have reached the final stage of adding goods at retail. Meanwhile producing firms already functioning normally will be able to realize from their sales more money than they have incurred as money costs and expenses. This sequence conceivably might go on and on repeatedly as the result of continuing enlargement of commercial bank loans and of deposits outstanding. There is no intention here to deny that newly created bank money might often be used to further production. Such use does not in any way deny that money profits can and are recorded as a result.

However, often bank loans have been made, during the last six decades or so, directly to consumers who, as an immediate result, are able to spend more than they have received as incomes through the cost payments made by profits-pursuing business firms. For example, the outstanding installment credit in the U.S. at the end of 1984 is reported in the *Federal Reserve Bulletin* of Sept. 1985, p. 40, Table 1.55, to have been $460.5 "B"illion, up by about 20% from $373.7 "B"illion at the end of 1983. Consumers seem to have spent in 1984 about $87 "B"illion they did not have. Some of the increase in installment "credit" was supplied by commercial bank loans that enlarged the outstanding money supply although the amount of increase from that source is uncertain. The installment credit outstanding held by commercial banks increased in 1984 by almost $41 "B"illion while that held by "finance companies" (which often borrow from banks) rose by a little under $10 "B"illion.

On the other hand, commercial banks during these last several decades have seriously invaded the preserve of "thrift institutions." Accordingly some portion of the increased total of consumer installment "credit" held by commercial banks and by finance companies might have been supplied by the re-lending of savings rather than by simply creating new and added bank money.

Occasionally an explanation raises more questions than it answers, as can be illustrated in the first set of assumptions used in this last postscript. In exploring the results of bank-created money destined to set available but idle resources to work producing goods and services, how can one explain the existence of such accumulated idle resources, especially unemployed labor? If the free enterprise system were to work the way in theory it is supposed to work, there would be no unemployed labor (except for "frictional unemployment"). If one cannot find an explanation that makes unemployment of labor a norm naturally to be expected in a well run free enterprise system, if there theoretically ought to be full employment of resources up to as much as the "normal" whole of the labor force can keep going, then under full employment what must be the effects of commercial bank creation of added money which, on being lent to borrowers, is inserted by them into the circulation to help finance production? Finally, what about the great concept known as "forced saving"?

CHAPTER 7

Enter: Financial Spasms in Leading Free Enterprise Areas Beginning in 1720s

An astute reader likely will recognize that the ups-and-downs, the prosperities-and-depressions, that are the focus in this chapter are what economists long have called "business cycles." However, that traditional name is somewhat inaccurate, for there need be no true regularity in those swings, either in amplitude or periodicity. And it might be, too, that the word "business" is misleading, for there can be considerable divergence in the mind's-eye meaning transmitted to the reader when one says "business" cycle. The spasms of irregular alternations between prosperity and depression in fact are basically financial. Let them be known, for accuracy in analysis, as financial spasms.

Likely it will be beneficial, also, if there is a clear distinction between financial spasms and other kinds of economic catastrophes. This may be done by characterizing the unusual nature of the financial depressions that have been suffered at intervals in leading free enterprise areas these last two and one-half centuries or a bit more. Throughout human history, economic difficulties have plagued human beings from time to time; and famines may be taken as the most severe and most self-evident of those great catastrophes. The contrast between famines and depressions can be described symbolically in a way to make the basic difference strikingly clear. A famine occurs because in an area of this planet there is a marked shortage of food, and many humans starve, likely even to death. On the other hand, a depression occurs, symbolically, because there are too many want-satisfying things available, including food, and many humans starve, some even to death. The catastrophe is a financial one, not one in terms of a shortage of physical things to satisfy wants nor even in terms of available resources with which to produce more (including food) if only those people in need were possessed of sufficient money purchasing power. During a depression a significant fraction of the population goes hungry and is ill-housed and ill-clothed even while there is an abundance of physical resources, including labor, to turn out more of nearly everything that is desired.

Wesley C. Mitchell and the research associates he assembled beginning in 1919 at the National Bureau of Economic Research concluded that the very first of the situations that truly manifested the characteristics of a depression appeared in the 1720s, primarily in Western Europe. Depressions have continued to occur off and on in the financially leading free enterprise nations ever since.

As the reader holds the foregoing facts and dates clearly in mind, recall that money-creating banking was given unwittingly "the spark of life" by that "Forced Loan of 1640." In that "loan," the King of England borrowed on his initiative alone the money that wealthy merchants in London had left, in accord with a usage that had evolved, for safekeeping overnight in The Tower. After their funds vanished, the merchants began to engage for the purpose of money safekeeping, when their enterprises were closed, the services of the strongboxes and watchmen of the London goldsmiths. It soon turned out that the coin-of-the-realm brought to the goldsmiths by London merchants continued largely to lie idle in the hands of those various goldsmiths. The merchants found it convenient to make payment by giving to some payees either goldsmiths' receipts (which became banknotes) or negotiable-orders-of-withdrawal (which turned out to be checks) on their goldsmith deposits. When various goldsmiths began to succumb to the temptation to lend some of that "idle" money that really were deposits of the merchants, they soon discovered that borrowers commonly wished to take the proceeds of their loans in goldsmith receipts or as deposits against which they, themselves, could write checks. The "idle" coin-of-the-realm money continued to seem to lie largely idle and unused, even though title to some of it was being transferred. Coin actually become "reserves" in the main. The goldsmiths, by moving along essentially in step and at a modest cadence, could lend more and more and still more — until these reserves, in relative terms, had become so small as to be merely "safe" in the sense of being only sufficient to make sure they could provide adequate redemption if and when demands for redemption occasionally might be made.

Now ponder the history of John Law (Scottish "financier," 1671-1729) who, after having been denied permission to do so in England, finally in the late 1710s gained consent of the French government to float a bank there. There he issued paper money to "take over" or buy up and "fund" the national debt. He used bank-created funds to help with colonization and commerce in the Mississippi country of North America. This eventuated in a "Big Time for a Little While," as the Mississippi Bubble burst with a bang in the early 1720s.

Note that the English, closely following John Law's Mississippi Scheme, had a scheme of their own. The South Sea Scheme also involved the taking over and funding of the national debt by the South Sea Company which was to be given a monopoly of the trade with the South Sea area. Indeed, 1720 brought great speculation and became known as the South Sea Year. But the South Sea Bubble also burst in the early 1720s, in part because of fraud by its managers.

To anyone who has grasped the true nature of the money-making objective of mercantilistic-type business, its natural origin and development and its dominance now in the 1980s in the U.S., those aspects that truly are important, such as total output either in money volume or physical volume and of employment of the labor force (even though the little enterprises, which usually do not really need to make money, may number upward of forty times as many), the occurrence of business financial spasms need be no mystery. Profits-pursuing firms, that in producing require to be large in order to attain adequate efficiency and to survive competitively, nearly invariably must raise considerable money to use as capital funds. They must disburse from those capital funds money to meet costs and expenses. And after the lapse of time needed to complete production (which latter involves a time-consuming flow from the very first extraction of materials until goods are available for sale at retail), they must strive to realize selling prices which are greater than the cost and expenses properly allocated to the items sold. As the money payments made by business firms (which payments actually are driplets concurrently dripping off at each of the several junctures of production) move on the whole only as fast as output flows in the opposite direction through the several steps, the incomes created by the business disbursements total only the equal of the cost of the output coming to market. If potential buyers were to spend their entire incomes, and if the entire output were sold, profits-seeking firms would not make any money on the whole. However, some might gain to the extent that others lose, the latter by failing to recover as much as they have paid out.

However, if there is inserted into that portrayal a significant addition to the amount of money circulating, either by new money being created by commercial banking operations (as loans operations are made at a faster pace than others are paid) or somehow by causing money to flow into the nation net from abroad, so that the total increases, buyers of end-products can spend for goods more money than businesses collectively have furnished them as incomes. It makes very little or no difference where in the goods and service flow or the consumption juncture the new borrowing (i.e., lending) occurs. It doesn't matter where the added money is inserted. There is always a seller who stands earlier. Money profit naturally will eventuate in the accounts of sellers who are prior in the production sequence.

There is another possible aspect to the money-making that results. It seems to me that the insertion of added, newly created bank money may yield a series of money profits to each of several sellers who stand earlier in sequence in the producing chain. Possibly the first seller who realizes some mercantilistic-type, chrematistic profit when the newly added money first is spent will retain a portion to finance expansion and will use some to distribute as dividends. It seems that the whole still will flow on to enable those next sellers antecedent in the production chain to record some net profit, considered collectively. However, this involves an analysis of some uncertainty and on which assistance is requested.

Ponder another sense in which the injection of new, added money into the circulation may give rise to a series of successive recordings of profits in the accounts of big firms. If and to the extent that new money injected into the circulation yields the appearance of money profits which latter then are distributed as dividends, the latter's circulation again can result in the recording of net earnings a second time. For example, since there can be little or no doubt that an enlargement of the money in circulation almost inevitably will generate profit of at least equal amount in business accounting records, if the whole of those profits thus given birth be distributed as dividends and the whole thereof be spent completely for consumer goods, it seems that such added money could go around the circle again and give birth to an equal amount of business profits another time. This, however, also is a concept which awaits further analysis and clarification and on which aid is invited.

Nonetheless, clearly a big portion of whatever profits are born through the process of injecting new money into the circulation likely will be retained to finance business expansion and a considerable fraction of what is distributed as dividends will be invested directly by recipients into financing business expansion. Hence my guesstimate is that the total financial profits recorded in the collective accounts of business will come out to only two, three or four times the amount of additional money injected into the circulation. After some such multiple, the whole will be absorbed into a higher level of total costs.

However, there are at least two additional mechanisms that easily are identified which by enlargement also give rise to the appearance of profits in business accounting records, supplementary to that prime one of the injection of added money into the circulation. Reference is to increase in outstanding open-book-account credit on the one hand and to the piling of inventory on the other. To the extent that in selling the output, sellers realize prices which absorb the whole of the incomes of potential buyers and in addition extend to the latter additional credit (the other side of which is consumer debt), prices can be agreed upon that appear on the average to exceed the purchasing power that the producing processes have generated. In a comparable way, if inventories are increased, with only a tiny fraction of output being held back to augment accumulated inventory, the rest which is sold can be at prices which on the average exceed the costs and expenses properly attributed to them. In any case it seems clear that the profit recorded as the result of either of these two supplementary expansions will be only in a 1-to-1 ratio with the amount of any increase. There is no ground for expecting any multiplier effect, unlike expansion of the money in circulation.

Let the three elements that have been described as resulting in the recording of mercantilistic-type profits or chrematistics profits be characterized in this backhanded way: We know that all three of them tend to be expanded during a typical period of prosperity. What is being described here is the fact that their expansion can be absorbed in no other way into the accounts of business except that they cause growth in the money value of business assets, therefore in the recording of the kind of profits which big businesses naturally have come to seek as their controlling goal in producing. An addition to the money supply in circulation, that most important financial expansion, likely seems to yield business profits to the extent of some low-number multiple while the secondary or supplementary increases in outstanding (undiscounted) book credit and accumulation of added inventory yield the appearance of profits in ratio of only 1-to-1.

It has been said earlier that if new money is inserted into the circulation, business profits of the type naturally sought by big, free enterprise firms will be recorded. It can be assimilated in no other way. There can be differences of utmost importance in the *kind* (or "quality") of money which is added. If within the nation itself there is production of significant quantities of precious metal(s) used as standard money, such added new money-metal can be injected into the circulation with essentially beneficial effects, especially if found or produced by a large number of independent prospectors. Or, if less developed free enterprise areas are producers of important amounts of precious metals used as standard money in leading financial areas, acquisition of such money or metals by the latter through favorable balances of trade (or payments) can be beneficial in the main. But favorable balances for the developed areas that drain the less-developed areas of their basic, acceptable money stock must culminate in time in dire results. This surely will come to a termination and will cause prosperity to cease. No serious depression need result, but the prosperity previously enjoyed will dwindle. The money in circulation can be enlarged also by a sovereign government's issuing paper money. If that be fully and undoubtedly redeemable in coin of the realm of unchanging weight and fineness, there need be little trouble created. Of course, the increase in such paper money is strictly limited in amount because of the maintenance of redemption. If government-printed paper money be irredeemable and is not strictly limited to a modest amount, it soon will depreciate markedly and lead to dire consequences. The technique for increasing the money in circulation that is the focus of attention here is the bank creation of money. This now is mainly demand deposits that circulate by checks that pass through the clearing processes, as in the U.S. today.

Historically, the ability of our commercial banks to create added money has been restrained by the leash of the requirement that demand deposits (or bank notes, now confined to Federal Reserve Notes) be backed by reserves some part of which had to be standard money. So long as bank-created added money was tied tightly to reserves ostensibly available for the former's redemption when demanded, and so long as those reserves included standard money of a fixed weight and fineness, and so long as one holding bank notes or bank demand deposits could request and obtain standard coin in exchange, there was a limit beyond which the banking system could not reasonably expand the amount of such money in circulation. Accordingly, over a period of years our commercial banks would tend, rather gradually, to build up our money supply, by increasing the amount of their loans outstanding, until they had gone about as far as they were premitted. However that upper limit itself might be able to grow to some extent as more standard money (or such precious metal) was added to the reserves. Nonetheless, by gradually increasing loans outstanding our banks tended in the course of a few years to approach the permissible limit. Then an undesirable reaction naturally tended to set in.

Since it was inescapable that sellers as a whole will have been showing profits as the money supply in circulation was expanded through growth in outstanding loans made by commercial banks, so it will be inevitable that the rate and/or amount of profits made collectively will shrink as money enlargement is slowed down to a halt. However, some firms will continue to show some net earnings because others incur some losses by failing to realize current selling price as large as their current costs and expenses. Moreover, as some of the dividends that are distributed likely will be spent for consumer goods, they will tend to yield business profits again in the next circulation. Hence even if bank creation of new money ceases entirely (say banks have expanded to the limit permitted by reserve requirements), business recording of net earnings likely will shrink gradually through several circulations before they finally decline in aggregate to zero. If this is all that happens it might be possible to assume that business simply descends to a condition of making no money collectively so that a period of stagnation-recession sets in.

But something more is likely to follow and a period of recession longer than a few months is highly improbable. Almost naturally the situation is apt to get "worse" or to get "better."

Consider first a historical case in which at the start of a recession which promised to descend into full-scale depression a surprising change took place that turned things for the better (from the standpoint of big profit-seeking firms). In the early 1890s, in the U.S., the stage seemed completely set for a depression following a recession. However, then discoveries were made of gold in South Africa and in the Klondike area of northwest Canada and in Alaska. There followed remarkable production; in the twenty years following 1892, the gold produced in the world amounted to several times as much (around four times as much, if memory serves well) as had been produced through the whole four centuries following the discovery of the New World in 1492 (and let it be remembered that much money and precious metals had been taken out of the Americas in early decades). As one result our U.S. banks soon acquired markedly increased reserves, and the incipient recession/depression was cut short.

At the other extreme, the more likely case is that recession will degenerate into depression, if bank lending which enlarges money supply has reached nearly its limit and reserves are not somehow increased. A depression involves more or less liquidation rather than merely a stagnant level of little or no realization of profit in the collective or macrochrematistic sense. If recession has set in because money-creating lending banks have gone up to about their limit and cease further expanding, some borrowers likely will find themselves unable to pay off, even if all of their prior intentions and operations have been honest. Some minor fraction of borrowers or lenders likely will be found to have acted fraudulently, thus making the situation worse. Loan losses for many of the banks inevitably will be suffered.

Even if all financial operations have been completely ethical, any attempt by any bank creditors to collect on and reduce net some of their outstanding loans or any attempt on the parts of some of the debtors to pay off and shrink bank loans (that earlier have augmented the money in circulation) necessarily will subtract from the amount left of current consumer incomes that can be used to purchase the current output. Hence, producing firms will discover that it is impossible to recover from their sales as much as the costs and expenses they have incurred in turning out the items they have for sale. Since any debtors paying off some of those loans that earlier helped to create added money will work to decrease the money that remains in circulation, that must eventuate in negative net earnings on the whole for mercantilistic-type, chrematistic firms. Moreover, when once begun in any significant degree, this movement works like a snowball rolling downhill.

Some of the weaker banks likely will become "bankrupt" and add further to the slide. An almost continuous series of sequential insolvency on the parts of some of the financially weaker firms, and the tendency for an almost continuous rise in unemployment, will bring on progressive defaults on consumer debts.

To this juncture the discussion has concerned what happens when banks are limited by required reserves that include specification of a fixed minimum of standard money held somewhere. But the upper limit on creation of bank-money is a very different thing if reserves specifications are altered so as to require the inclusion of no standard money of any sort. Even here in the U.S. we recently have stooped to such an arrangement. In the mid-1960s and the early 1970s, in order to avoid the then existing restraints, we removed the last vestiges of redemption of other money into gold, even in international transactions. Since then legal monetary reserves have been confined to deposits on the books of the Federal Reserve Banks, and have been increasable by Federal Reserve action by that system's buying government debt obligations on the open market. Now there is no true limit on bank-creation of money except the wisdom and the will of money managers or the fright that could induce us to revert to barter, or money's decline in value so great as to bring on devaluation or even complete worthlessness and rejection and disuse and the "starting over" with a "new issue."

It is enlightening to recognize that, once the processes of pumping up the money in circulation by way of adding more and more bank-created money have begun, the rise thereof to its upper limit naturally tends to be irregular. It tends to be in a series of "fits-and-starts" as we move from plateau to plateau. Such plateaus generally are characterized as recessions. Recessions are pauses on the way up so long as a fixed limit has not been virtually reached or closely approached. Recessions or pauses on a climb of any sort are quite natural. We find it necessary to rest and "catch our breath" and really to adjust to and become accustomed to each higher level. Are there any among us who has not found himself pausing and "regrouping" before becoming reconciled to a recently boosted level of prices or to his first taking on a significantly increased amount of debt? Is there one among us who, in thinking back, is not somewhat amazed at the fact that after a time he takes the higher prices or his increased burden of debt as being a normal matter of course? And companion questions can be asked of those on the other sides of such transactions. Even though the trend may be upward, recessions along the way are usual even if a positive limit is not yet becoming any restraint.

How does the financial expansion get started up again, once the stagnant trough of a depression has been reached? Let this question be answered in terms of some historical examples. The stagnation and incipient depression of the early 1890s here in the U.S. was headed off and turned around by those discoveries of great new gold-producing areas and the resulting rapid expansion of the required reserves of our commercial banks during the two decades prior to the start of the first World War. Again The Great Depression that began in 1929 dragged on at a low level for several years. In the mid-1930s, we devalued the gold dollar in the sense that by reducing the amount of that metal specified as making a dollar to about 59% of what it long had been we instantly increased the gold reserves held by our banks by more than two-thirds. Banks thereafter could start lending much more again. In the mid-1960s, when our banks began to suffer the restraint of reserve requirements as the limiting factor, we removed the last vestiges of obligation of any sort that gold be included as part of commercial bank or central bank reserves. Thereafter the money-creating banking process has been held in check only by the wisdom and the will of the members of the

Federal Reserve Board or by our circulating money's descent in value towards worthlessness.

One final note, scarcely more than a postscript: Whereas the description in the foregoing several paragraphs has been confined to the curtailment of the expansion of bank-created money and in depression some actual liquidation thereof, the downward processes are augmented to a minor extent by the cessation of the accumulation of undiscounted open book credit on the one hand and by the cutting down on the piled-up inventories on the other hand. Firms are doubly willing to add to their inventories when prices are rising and are expected to continue to rise, but become very eager to liquidate drastically during any recession or depression. The ups and downs of these two factors are relatively small in comparison to the amount of bank money created in a strong prosperity and extinguished in a severe depression. But the rise and fall of open book credit and of inventories may have some special influence in determining the timing, particularly of a recession or a depression.

Business financial spasms (nee business cycles) are caused mainly by periods of non-saved-credit debt-inflation yielding general business profits, each period followed by one of debt-deflation yielding general business losses. Moreover, because production is dominated progressively ever more by large firms which, having absentee owners, must realize profits in the corporate-law and corporate-accounting sense to reward those absentee owners with profits dividends in order to be "successful," the increased pervasiveness and growing average size of our producing firms means that in time the magnitude of our financial spasms tends to become more violent. And because we have become more sophisticated in recent decades in creating non-saved-credit money and recently have removed the final constraint of any tie of money to precious metals, the length of the periods of our spasms can be expected to be considerably stretched and their magnitudes and severity still further enlarged.

Should we here in the U.S. suffer soon the super-depression herein predicted to be imminent (unless we hasten some relevant changes) it is to be hoped that such depression is not blamed on outsiders, *e.g.*, not labeled an evil "communist conspiracy." The cause is to be found in the free enterprise system itself, in the objective that large business firms naturally pursue, in the financial institutions we have evolved, and in the way those institutions function. Our financial spasms, usually called business cycles, have been recurring ever since the 1720s and antedate modern communism by about two centuries.

CHAPTER 8

Some Automatic Pumps That Puff Up Our "Debt-Inflation"

Every reader should ponder that in this chapter the term "debt-inflation" is used, described and analyzed in contrast to "price-inflation." It is the former which signifies something of great importance and disturbing effects, rather than the latter. Prices on the whole and on the average, as measured by a well-constructed series of index numbers, may be caused to rise or to decline by each of many different forces. They may even move in the opposite direction from debt-inflation. But during any period in which we experience considerable debt-inflation (even if prices on the average may be moving along essentially unchanged or actually declining), our financial system is sinking into a morass of difficulties.

In this chapter price-inflation refers to a rise in prices in general (or on the average) as indicated by some appropriate measure. But debt-inflation as used here is intended to refer to the increase of debts outstanding as the result of enlarging the outstanding amount of "non-saved" credit extended to borrowers. This is overwhelmingly in connection with those commercial banking operations which create added money that is inserted into the circulation.

To clarify the above distinction it is useful to identify two very different types of credit, namely, "saved credit" and "non-saved credit." Saved credit comes into existence when recipients of incomes choose to spend or directly invest in end-products somewhat less than the total money purchasing power they have received. Instead, they lend their savings to others, to borrowers, who will use the funds for spending or investing. Often such savings are accumulated along with savings of others in a thrift institution, which on behalf of the savers makes the loan(s) and extends the credit. The total amount of purchasing power brought to the market is unchanged; some portion of incomes is simply transferred from savers to borrowers. In reverse, on repayment, the amount of buying power that flows back in the opposite direction simply relocates purchasing power. There is no change in the total in the hands of potential buyers. Neither the extension of such saved credit nor its repayment alters the amount that collectively can be laid out to purchase end-products.

However, non-saved credit is a wholly different thing. Typically it arises when a commercial banking operation takes place and, without any equivalent prior saving, the lender (bank) accepts a debt obligation of a borrower and in exchange creates for him an added demand deposit against which that borrower can draw checks. The checks will move in the clearings to the checking accounts of those others to whom payments are being made. It is usually said that the lending bank has "extended credit." Of course the other side of such a transaction is that the borrower has gone into debt. It is the building up of more and more of this non-saved credit that provides the appearance of financial "prosperity" and eventually gets our financial system into very big trouble when we stop expanding its outstanding total and try to reduce or liquidate much of it. Of course when we no longer include a significant proportion of standard money, coin or bullion in our banks' reserves, the debt-inflation may be carried on and on.

To make the contrast between price-inflation and debt-inflation more vivid, note that twice here in the U.S. since 1872 we have experienced debt-inflation while prices were declining or were standing almost still. It is likely that we may be doing this again in the mid-1980s to a far greater extent that ever before, except possibly in our "Wildcat Banking" period of 1836-63. From 1873 until the early 1890s, our U.S. prices trended downward gradually, so much that twentieth-century economists have remarked upon what a dreary and adverse period that must have been. But Alfred Marshall, English economist who originated the Neo-Classical system of economic theory in the 1880s, early in this twentieth century testified before a committee of Parliament that, contrary to the notion assumed by many recent economists as they look back, the 1870s and 1880s were very good years. Actually in the U.S. we were expanding bank credit and increasing our money supply fast enough to enable our business firms to sell their output quite profitably. However prices moved downward because we were industrializing at a great rate following the Industrial Revolution in England and the stimulus of our Civil War, so output was increased rapidly and our unit costs were caused to fall. Prices were not declining as fast nor as much as costs. Hence profits aided by debt-inflation but not price-inflation were satisfactory. Similar industrialization was taking place in Western Europe while England continued to scurry along on the route discovered and explored there a few decades earlier.

The second period of rising debt-inflation devoid of price-inflation here in the U.S. was that of 1923-29. Between "wholesale prices" and "the cost of living" series of index numbers, one moved along almost horizontal while the other trended downward gradually. It was believed to be "a new era." Yet every knowledgeable person senses that during those seven years we in this nation were somehow inflating, and one knows, too, what happened when we reached a limit to our debt-inflation (without price-inflation). One also knows what happened when we attempted to liquidate some of that debt-inflation. In the last two-thirds of the 1920s productivity improvements caused output to grow and unit costs to decline faster than the rate of increase in non-saved credit.

One should study the current rise of our U.S. debt-inflation (say since 1965). We have experienced greater amounts of such inflation than during any time since our Civil War. True, in the 1970s we did experience considerable price-inflation, but in quite recent years we have suffered very great debt-inflation along with little or only modest price-inflation. Likely our unfavorable balances of payments owed foreigners have had much to do with creating what seems to be an anomaly. The reader is cautioned to keep a sharp watch regarding the considerable rise in our debt-inflation, now that bank-money is being created without the limitation of any sort of standard money being required as part of bank reserves.

Several automatic pumps puff up our debt-inflation by helping along the expansion and accumulation of outstanding non-saved credit, extended by commercial bank operations, which results in increasing our money supply.

1. *The Labor Union Wage-Increase Pump*: Since that portion of output which profit-pursuing business firms hope to sell to wage earners is priced a bit above costs and expenses in order for sellers to make money, workers cannot buy everything offered them simply via spending the money incomes they have received. Either some of the product destined for and offered to them must be held back and added to business inventories or, instead, many workers must sink, further and further, into debt. Assume that the money value ascribed to the added inventory on the one hand plus

the added debt undertaken by the wage earners together total 8%. On the whole the chrematistic sellers should be able to record 8% profit. Assume then that this is repeated through each of two or three production cycles so that the value of the goods held back plus the accumulated indebtedness of the workers becomes 8% at the end of the first production cycle, 16% at the end of the second cycle, 24% at the end of the third cycle, et cetera. It is likely that in time the workers will form a union intended to enable members to acquire the goods just beyond their financial reach and to escape from the worry of growing debt. If there are only a few firms producing the same or similar things, the new union must make sure that the workers in those competing firms are unionized too. Then the wage-earning employees in each firm, or jointly in all competing firms, will demand the right to bargain collectively. They will strive to obtain higher wages which they hope and believe will enable them to buy those items that sellers have been urging on them. They hope also to pay off and get out from under the worry as well as the debt they did incur on the purchases already made. From here the process starts all over again. Often the employer, finding himself in need of more "working capital" in order to meet higher wage bills, will borrow such funds from commercial banks. Those banks extend non-saved credit and create added money in the process. As any such employer uses his borrowings to cover his enlarged total wage bill his costs and expenses to be allocated to each unit of output will rise, assuming no change in efficiency or productivity. However, even if there is improvement, an altered line of analysis applies which ends with the same result. It follows that he will raise his asking price accordingly. So again the workers will find themselves short of receiving sufficient incomes to enable them to buy that output which sellers hope somehow to foist upon them. The wage earners are not being "exploited" in the Marxian sense. They are being made victims in only the financial or chrematistics sense. Goods and services are not being withheld from workers with any evil intention. The producing firms really are eager that employees as a whole buy more and more goods. The latter simply are short of income-created purchasing power. And a union attempt to acquire the needed additional purchasing power, if successful, leads the employer to borrow, at least in prosperous times, non-saved credit that increases the debt-inflation.

A few qualifications are indicated. First, if wage rate increases are won by big and strong unions, non-union wages are likely in time to follow upward. Second, wage rates on the whole could not possibly be raised through round after round if (with the number of employed workers as least as great as before) employers simply rely on borrowing the savings that people make voluntarily out of their incomes.

2. *The Indexation Pump*: This operates most effectively when it is once started by some significant price inflation. But once it has become an accepted and customary thing, it tends to operate very much as a perpetual motion machine, since each guaranteed increase of certain incomes to match the average of the rise in consumer prices will help to make sure that prices will rise again and require another increase in those incomes geared to match.

To clarify, assume that there is little or no improvement in efficiency or productivity and little or no resulting increase in output accompanied by lower unit costs. Big producers, striving for money profits, mark up their asking price per unit above the costs and expenses. The latter action could be expected to boost prices a few percentage points. Potential buyers who enjoy indexed incomes will be entitled to have their incomes increased somehow. Whoever is obligated to disburse the added money, either in increased wages of production workers or government employees or pensions of private firms or government retirees or elderly people "on social security," will be compelled to lay out an increased amount of money. Even if not at first, sooner or later those payers will turn to borrowing additional non-saved credit of the variety that enables our commercial-banking operations to further increase the money supply outstanding in circulation. Increased spending on the parts of recipients who receive the increased incomes will help set the stage for another round. This can continue, it seems to me, round after successive round with little tendency to diminish.

However, the above requires to be qualified too, because if the additional money for indexed incomes is disbursed without resort to borrowing added non-saved credit (as by the raising of added taxes or by the borrowing solely of savings), the pump described above will not function — and indexation likely will prove unnecessary.

One can construct a good case in the interest of equity and fair play for indexing many kinds of incomes. However, once cranked up, indexation tends to run on and on, often at an ever increasing pace, until some limit is reached, as devaluation at first, then eventually as default. The process can be kept rolling solely because some power somewhere is exercised that keeps enlarging the money supply (in foreign lands as well as the U.S.), either by commercial banking or a government's printing more and more money, or some of both.

3. *The Agricultural Subsidy Pump*: The focus here is on small agricultural operations, or "family farms." They should be thought of essentially as households striving "to get a living." In general, big producing firms that buy products from such farmers and/or others who sell to such farmers invariably try to buy cheaply and to sell dearly. Again and again, almost always through the last several decades, our millions of farm families have experienced difficulty in obtaining enough money from sale of their output to enable them to cover their business expenses and also their expenses for a satisfactory standard of living. The prices they receive are either "too low" or the prices they pay (for

farm operation and for family living) are "too high." Actually the small farmers are struggling to maintain their existence in competition with the big firms entering this preserve with tractors and other large and costly machinery driven by inanimate power and the purchase of fertilizer and water. So the small farmers have sought the aid of government and, out of sympathy and because those citizens have many political votes, the federal government here in the U.S. has responded by providing diverse production subsidies as well as crop restriction techniques. Each year the cost to our government is many billions of dollars. Most, if not all, of those billions can be thought of as being connected to deficit spending. Much of those funds comes first into our treasury's hands through the increase of non-saved credit which helps to augment our money supply. This occurs even though our commercial banking system may acquire the increased government debt obligations somewhat later and through open market operations. If subsidies were supplied by using taxes or by resort to saved-credit only, this pump would not cause debt-inflation.

4. *The Foreign Aid Pump* is like that of agricultural subsidies. However, further description of it and its operation is delayed until the next chapter, Ch. 9.

5. *The Borrowing Against Increased Capital-Value Pump*: As we enlarge our supply of money in circulation, enabling buyers of end-products to augment their incomes enough to purchase the whole output from big producers at prices which on average yield the latter satisfactory net profit, certain capital assets are likely to rise in value. This is doubly true of assets such as land and non-renewable resources which latter become more difficult and more expensive to extract as well as more costly to find or reach. Accordingly, there is a considerable temptation, often encouraged by our banks, to borrow more and more against the heightened money value of such assets and to use the added

money to venture further or elsewhere, or even simply to speculate. This recalls to mind the scheme of John Law and his Mississippi Bubble (French) and of the English South Sea Scheme in the 1710s and 1720s, as well as of Henry Ford's advocacy in his *Dearborn Independent* in the 1910s that we in the U.S. should issue money against land values. Obviously such operations, when tried, spiral up and up and up, usually to a crash into worthlessness. But they can be tried only to the extent that some group has somehow acquired the power to create more and more money. Any reasonable limit on this will terminate the debt-inflation and also the inescapable price-inflation.

6. *The "Take-Over" and/or Recapitalization Pump*: There is much actual similarity between expanded financing of a prosperous firm by the owner(s) and insiders of that firm and, instead, a "take-over" of a firm by outsiders. An analyst can ponder, as typical, a small firm which has been especially profitable, either due to general prosperity or because it offers unusual or especially good and highly desired products. In any case let one think of a venture which has attained an earning capacity markedly greater than sufficient to yield adequate earnings on the market value of its capital securities outstanding (or, if none of the latter, then on the money capital actually invested). The prior owner may decide to "recapitalize" by going to some financial market to offer new "securities" that total much more than the money ever inserted as capital funds. Brokers likely will underwrite the new issue and at the close of a selling period will buy up any unsold "securities," at a bit of a discount to be sure. Likely whatever portion of the new capital obligations are thus "assumed" by the brokerage firms will be pledged to secure the needed funds, commonly non-saved debt-inflating money. Many of the final buyers of the new "securities," whether purchased before the termination selling date or afterward from the brokers' inventories, also will resort to the borrowing of some non-saved, money-creating, debt-inflation

"funds." But the prior owner(s) more likely than not will retain some ownership instruments and maintain partial, if not full, control.

There will be only a slight difference if outsiders "take over" a firm, in contrast to mere recapitalization by the prior owner(s). Often (if a hostile take-over) the acquirer(s) will have had to arrange in advance sufficient bank borrowings (i.e., no doubt non-saved debt-inflating credit) so that they can pay some cash for the capital "securities" they need in order to gain control. Then they likely will issue a sufficient number of capital obligations through which they will recover their whole actual outlay — and yet have left for themselves capital obligations of much monetary worth (but possibly devoid of any actual money outlay by them) and often of control as well.

Recapitulation Chapters 1 thru 8

Summary Especially
for Economists

This must begin with recognition that what follows is based on a fundamentally different foundation from that which all systems of economic theory since Adam Smith's day have accepted as descriptive of laissez-faire free enterprise. That universal foundation-assumption that underlies every "orthodox" theory, but which is alleged here to be essentially false and mistaken, is the belief that the financing of the processes of production always creates for potential buyers of end-products aggregate incomes, or purchasing power, equal to the total prices (or "value") of the goods turned out. Therefore, conventionally it is reasoned that if the whole of such incomes simply is devoted with reasonable dispatch to purchase the products, goods, and services, that result (including what is saved being used, directly or indirectly, to buy the newly finished capital goods), the whole of demand and supply would come out even — and all would be right with the laissez faire economy (and the world).

It is the above notion that here is being denied and appraised as being false and fatally mistaken in fact when taken as descriptive of reality of private free enterprise. However, before this work embarks on further development of criticism of that notion and the assumption that it helps explain free enterprise, let attention be focused on my allegation that "ALL" accredited systems of theory purporting to describe and explain laissez faire are firmly founded on it.

First, every well-schooled economist will recognize that mentioned idea as the necessary first premise in Say's "Law of Markets," formulated and asserted by J.B. Say very early in the 1800s as he labored to better organize and explain and popularize what he understood Adam Smith to have said and to have meant. For the benefit of any non-economist who reads this summary, Say's "Law . . ." is the allegation that supply creates demand (sellers use the money they obtain for what they relinquish to buy other items they desire, instead). It is concluded that demand therefore is always equal to supply, and there can be no general overproduction (although unbalanced production is possible). And it is held that, for facility in economic analysis, money can be dropped out of consideration. The first and underlying premise in Say's "Law . . ." is that those who participate in production invariably receive money incomes sufficient to enable them to purchase the whole output if those incomes be devoted properly to that end.

Second, it appears that no economist ever offered any criticism of J.B. Say's necessary underlying assumptions during the (approximate) century and a third following its initial presentation. It seems to have come under some doubt for the first time when J.M. Keynes' *General Theory...* was published in 1935. But Keynes' criticism was a very different aspect and not that of Say's basic first or underlying assumption. Keynes was certain and asserted in his book that potential buyers always receive money incomes as the result of participating in production sufficient to purchase the whole output. But he reasoned that as a result of progress eventuating in higher average incomes and lower rates of interest, income recipients would save more and more and would be less and less attracted to putting portions of those savings back into circulation with ordinary dispatch. He reasoned, also, that savers would hold more and more of their enlarged savings in liquid forms, since "liquidity" itself offers some potential advantages. He reasoned further that the holding liquid of more and more savings would curtail total demand and would bring on depression. But Keynes was sure beyond doubt that potential buyers always are supplied enough money incomes in return for their participation in production to create sufficient potential demand. This is proved positively by the following words, which he asserted as being a "proposition which is undubitable," in his sentence that begins on line 20 of page 20 of his *General Theory*...:

"...the income derived in the aggregate by all the elements in the community concerned in a productive activity necessarily has a value exactly equal to the *value* of the output."

Obviously Keynes did not question the adequacy of the total incomes generated in the course of financing production. Instead his view and his explanation of depressions was that for certain reasons as a result of progress people save more and more and for other reasons they hold more and more of their savings in liquid forms. Some observers have summarized the whole of his theory system in the allegation that there is "too much saving."

Third, as to the aggregate of incomes created in connection with production, "supply-side" economic theory is based on that same, identical assumption as is Say's Law and as is the "demand-side" economic theory of Keynes and his followers. *Wealth and Poverty* by George Gilder, published in 1981 by Basic Books, asserts the following on page 47:

"As Thomas Sewall has explained in two books..., the theorem, associated with the name of French economist Jean-Baptiste Say, essentially maintains that the sum of the wages, profits, and rents paid in manufacturing a good is sufficient to buy it. This does not mean that the same people who make a thing will necessarily buy it, but they could. The sum of money paid to the factors of production, chiefly in rents, wages, salaries, and profits, for making and marketing of an automobile, for example, is precisely enough to purchase it. Therefore, across an entire system, purchasing power and producing power can always balance; there will always be enough wealth in an economy to buy its products. There cannot be a glut of goods caused by inadequate total demand. Producers, collectively, in the course of production, create demand for their goods. This idea is obviously simplistic in many ways, but it bears a number of key economic truths and implications never refuted by Keynes or anyone else. These truths are the foundation of contemporary supply-side theory."

The reader will conclude, of course, that George Gilder and the "supply-side" theorists for whom he speaks are sure that the money payments made in connection with financing production naturally create aggregate incomes for potential buyers precisely sufficient to enable them to purchase the whole of the end-products. Gilder and his colleagues go on from there to present "trickle-down" conclusions and recommendations for virtually unregulated free enterprise, i.e., regulated only by laissez-faire competition.

Yet the truth is that Gilder's basic conclusion concerning the adequacy of money purchasing power created in financing production is proved flatly false. Twice in his description of the payments made in connection with production he has included "profits." But every knowledgeable person knows that, with reference to big firms which are corporations, "profit" that is made on an item of output is in fact not handled normally or legally as a money cost. Moreover, "big" firms dominate. In 1977 the 2.4% of U.S. business ventures each with revenues of $1,000,000 or more enjoyed at least 75% of total sales and employed fully 75% of the workers then holding jobs. All accountants who possess well-rounded insights in their profession know that profit made on an item by a firm big enough to use capital funds supplied by numerous "absentee owners" is not even recorded, let alone distributed as dividends, until after that item has been sold (for money or a promise to pay money) at a price that exceeds actual money costs and expenses. Every attorney who is well versed in corporate law knows that it is illegal to pay out dividends in the guise of profits-distribution by the use of capital funds. Nearly all of the leaders of big firms and of their boards of directors know, or at least sense, this restraint in corporate law and in the principles of accounting. Accordingly, the profit (if any) that is made by a major firm on a selected product, say an automobile, as cited by Gilder, cannot possibly be used to help provide the buying power to carry off that particular item. Of course if some profit has been made on the sale of earlier output, some of that may be used to help purchase the current item. However, this insight merely starts an analyst on a chase back in the search to discover where and how some first profit was realized. One, in order to be thorough, dare not simply make appealing assumptions, as has George Gilder.

What has been said above regarding restraints on distributions of corporate profits of itself raises the almost imponderable problem for writers, such as Gilder, as to how, with progress and output growth, the whole of profits are able to increase. It raises also the problem as to what the effects will be if a portion of the profits already recorded are "ploughed back in" to finance expansion (and increase total costs and expenses), as in prosperous times historically have been upwards of half of the earnings of large U.S. firms. Of course an analyst will encounter some exasperating puzzles if he tries, as George Gilder is obligated to try, to trace every aspect out exhaustively. For example, if one tries to reason that the auto dealers pay sufficient money to acquire their inventory that the auto manufacturers will make some profit which the latter can disburse as dividends that will help consumers buy the specified item at retail, the question arises as to where those auto dealers got hold of all of that money which they paid to the manufacturers. Clearly the final conclusion must be that the profit made on a unit of product does not and cannot supply part of the money incomes that can be used to help buyers purchase that item of end-product. In large-sized firms, the group that now is dominant, the profit on a specified unit is not, legally and customarily, treated as a money cost or expense.

The reasoning of economists that often has seemed to many to justify one's belief in the adequacy of money purchasing power generated by the money payments made in financing production is reasoning appropriate for describing, not modern business, but the operation of the weekly market during the Middle Ages in western Europe. The goods brought to the market usually by members of area families, of the serfs and the peasants and the craftsmen, had been produced usually from beginning to end by the efforts of household members. Hence the items offered as "supply" almost always involved no money costs to finance production. What money was available in a market was used simply to facilitate final exchanges, and it could "circulate" independently and completely each time it changed hands and could attain a velocity quite unrelated to the time span required for the production processes that included all of the steps of the making and the marketing of goods.

However, such a simplistic use of money (merely to facilitate the final exchanges of finished goods) changed fundamentally, as did the velocity of money, as soon as division of labor became truly significant and considerably more complex than mere specialization by family members within a household. Whenever and wherever division of labor to produce a good comes to involve a series of distinct steps carried out by members of distinct households, obviously a time span is required for completion of each item, and naturally money payments usually are required, and they will be made in the opposite direction as the products move forward step-by-step. Accordingly money comes as a result to be used as capital funds to finance production and, hence, to circulate in direction opposite to the goods flow. Payments are made quid pro quo as output moves forward toward final completion and sale. Money used as capital funds, being paid out to meet costs and expenses, takes on a circuit flow with a circuit velocity that matches the speed of the production of goods, from beginning to completion. Indeed, symbolically the whole can be visualized as goods moving forward on a production conveyor line motivated by the force of money moving contra in an adjacent pipeline which at each step powers the producing and drips off some money as exhaust driplets in payment. Driplet-payments are made concurrently at many stations along the production line and the sum of those simultaneous driplets equals the cost and expenses of the one item just then completed and marketed (or sold). In the 1980s, it is no longer necessary to struggle to gain recognition of the circuit flow and circuit velocity concepts since this finally has come to be accredited and standard in economic theory, starting in the 1920s.

It is my view that it has turned out to be a great tragedy that neither any of Adam Smith's disciples nor any critics have been in these last two centuries sufficiently objective or analytical to see and to develop in full the monetary and financial ramifications in his treatment of the division of labor in the production processes. Had Smith, or someone else, done so soon after 1776, that surely would have led to the insights, the diagnosis needed to enable us to alter our free enterprise system appropriately so as to forestall by making unnecessary many of the wars fought in diverse places over this earth during these last two centuries, as well as the spasms of prosperity and depression that have plagued Western Civilization. It would have disclosed that mercantilism, which began to appear following the Crusades, while a natural development of a laissez faire system, was born with a congenital defect that requires correction. Such correction is imperative if the free enterprise system is to survive much longer, say at most beyond the otherwise forthcoming catastrophic depression.

Let us cogitate the fundamental implications of Smith's first "example" of the benefits of division of labor in "a trifling manufacture," that of making straight pins, involving ten men working together on "about eighteen distinct operations" in what he sometimes called a "workhouse" and sometimes a "manufactory." When they exerted themselves, they could make among them about twelve pounds of pins in a day, which was about 48,000 pins per day. It was far more likely than not that one man among those ten owned that "workhouse" and the "indifferent" tools and machines with which the workers were accommodated. But ownership could have been a partnership with, but highly unlikely, each of the ten workers being an equal partner. (Surely the enterprise was not a corporation, that being a form of business organization to which Smith was very strongly opposed.) Let us assume that ownership of the workplace, tools, and machines, and materials was by one man, one of the ten. Accordingly that one owner of the plant and equipment must have had to raise some capital funds, his money savings or savings of relatives and friends, to be used to buy those fixed capital assets or to pay for their construction. Further, at the end of each day, or each week, or each fortnight, he surely must have had to pay money wages to the nine other workers. He scarcely could have paid each of them upwards of forty-eight hundred pins at the close of each day, or almost twenty-nine thousand pins at the end of each six-day week, or a bit less than fifty-seven thousand pins as wages each two weeks. If he paid them wages in cash, he obviously became the owner of the pin at the conclusion of the transaction. And his sales of the pins likely would be made later in job lots. Therefore, he must have found it necessary somehow to raise additional money to use as working capital funds in order to meet his wage bill (and the costs of materials and power, perhaps) prior to his receipt of money revenue from his sales. Smith described the pin-making he observed as beginning with one man drawing out the wire, another straightening it, and a third cutting it. So wire was the principal raw material, which must have been purchased from the owner of a different "workhouse" (which obviously involved the laying out of money capital funds) where workers were employed (whose wages also required disbursement of additional capital funds). And the wire-maker would have had to obtain the necessary steel (unless there were integration) from a still prior enterprise in what Smith could have described as a "great manufacture" (in contrast to his "trifling manufacture" label for pin-making). If that pin-manufacturing venture was a business which paid wages and material costs in money, rather than in kind, it surely required, too, additional capital funds to pay shipping costs to send 288,000 pins per week to one and next time to another wholesaler, or possibly 576,000 (maybe 2,400 "papers of pins") each fortnight. In due course the owner of the pin-making firm would expect to recover money, likely from those wholesaler-middlemen in exchange for the pins delivered.

No question, the making of straight pins referred to by Adam Smith required that capital funds be raised by which each of several sequential entrepreneurs could pay out money funds, some in connection with financing plant and equipment and some to meet the expenses of wages and of raw materials and supplies and for heat and power and light. Correspondingly, it was inescapable that such money then would circulate against the flow of production, from turning out the raw materials through all of the steps needed to dispose at last of the pins to final consumers at retail. A circuit flow of money eventuated with a circuit velocity equal to that of the production span required for the steps of marketing as well as those of the making.

Now let one realize that when any entrepreneur(s) or firm, such as Adam Smith's pin-maker, puts a significant amount of money into a production venture in order to meet money costs and expenses that will be incurred in carrying out the operations, it is natural that he covets the recovery of *more money* from sales than has been disbursed in connection with producing the item(s) sold. Indeed, it might be valid to assert that he (or they) necessarily must try to realize such augmented money revenue from sales. It is difficult or virtually impossible to conjure up any alternative first objective. To be sure, if one's business is very small, he might pay from his capital funds some wages to himself for the work he does and/or a salary for his managing activities. However, it would be quite ridiculous for him to pay himself profits-dividends out of his capital funds, because the latter was obviously assembled for use in meeting actual costs and expenses. Furthermore, sufficient funds should be retained on hand and available to assure the future payment of wages and for materials and to assure creditors generally that their claims will be met. Let one visualize himself as the pin-making entrepreneur in Adam Smith's illustration: What would you embrace as your primary goal? What outcome would enable you to feel adequately rewarded? What alternative objective could you establish for yourself different from that of trying to recover more money from your sales than the money costs and expenses you had met out of your capital funds?

Yet there is another approach that naturally leads to the same goal of trying to make money. Since the 1776 pin-making operation took full advantage of the state-of-the-art division of labor, it was many times more efficient and productive (according to Smith) than was possible for any inexperienced person trying to make pins for his individual household, and even far more pro-ductive than an experienced pin-maker who works alone in performing all operations himself, using the best of the available tools and machines. Therefore it seems that there will be no doubt that pins made by thorough-going division of labor will sell at prices which easily exceed the costs and expenses that have been incurred; these latter will be significantly lower than the "costs" that are saved the buyer who otherwise would have to make pins for himself. Competition actually is only with a few highly specialized manufactories with comparable efficiency; it is not with laissez-faire individuals. So it seems easily possible for such a producer-firm to set asking prices reasonably, or even unreasonably, above costs and expenses and naturally expect to find sufficient demand. The few competitors likewise seek to "make money."

Let the above be reinforced by assuming that in 1776 in the whole of Great Britain the need for pins may aggregate not more than the output of two hundred pin-makers of the type and size described by Smith, and that such size was the minimum required to take full advantage of the division of labor that the state of the art then provided. Each of those two hundred proprietors would have had the same need for raising capital funds as did that one described in . . .*The Wealth of Nations*; each would have found it necessary to pay out similar capital funds to meet costs and expenses for making pins. Each would then have had pins to sell. Each *naturally* would have hoped to recover more money in making sales than the costs and expenses he had incurred. Pin-making venturers would have found themselves competing with each other only, not with far less efficient individuals or households who might consider making pins. Insofar as their financial operations were concerned, their financing of production naturally would have failed to create incomes equal to the value of the output (value, as Keynes used that term, means selling price, per quotation supra). Of course this conclusion requires the embracing of the concept that money moves in a circle, the circuit flow description that came into our literature first in the 1920s (despite its actual existence since the time of well-developed mercantilism). Also, its circular velocity matches the counter flow of output. Such a flow is the reality, of course, as soon as division of labor causes production to be separated into a series of time-consuming steps that require money payments as costs and expenses.

The remainder of Adam Smith's short first chapter contains further description and discussion laudatory of division of labor, including explanation of the circumstances which he thought responsible for the resulting great increase in productivity and output. It then terminates with a final paragraph that contains a listing of the numerous steps he visualized as involved in the efficient making and supplying a woolen coat for a day-laborer, as coarse and rough as it may appear. This time he was treating a part of a "greater manufacture," in contrast to the "very trifling manufacture" of making straight pins. His description of the coat-making was carried all the way back, not simply to the growing and harvesting of the wool, but even the mining of ore and the burning of the charcoal used by the smelter to make the metal used in turning out the shears with which the shepherd was able to clip the wool (and other workers to make the more complicated machines). He listed the brick-maker and bricklayer who helps erect the smeltinghouse. Moving in the other direction he mentioned many of the steps involved in spinning, weaving, transporting, buying, and selling between steps. He mentioned the transporting to bring dyes from far places and the making of ships and sails and provisions and providing employment for sailors, et cetera, et cetera. These descriptions by Smith have been noted here to show that even in his day numerous steps (which take time) were involved in producing many items. At each of many junctures proprietors or firms, even in 1776, obviously had to be large and had to raise money capital funds from which to pay out money to meet costs and expenses. Such payments caused money to circulate quid pro quo against the flow of output, and each proprietor in making sales naturally strove (in order to "succeed") to recover more money than he had paid to meet his production costs and expenses. The financing of production when and where division of labor had become significant even in Smith's time obviously did not generate sufficient money incomes for potential buyers to equal or "cover" the desired selling price of the whole output: this denied "Say's Law."

The third chapter of . . . *The Wealth of Nations* explains that "division of labor is limited by the extent of the market." Smith described how water carriage cheapened the cost of transport, made broader the markets for many items and made more involved the division of labor. He explained that a great "broadwheeled wagon, attended by two men, and drawn by eight horses" could make a round trip between London and Edinburgh (Smith's base) in about six weeks and carry about four tons of freight each way. In contrast, "in about the same time a ship navigated by six or eight men, and sailing between the ports of London and Leith, frequently carries and brings back two hundred tons weight of goods." Mention is made of these operations, now recognized as "production" too, to point out and emphasize that Adam Smith ought to have pursued his views by analyzing and explaining the raising of money capital funds by the owner of a great "wagon" or of a ship and the use of money to finance the operation of those "wagons" or ships, and the replenishing of the money costs and expenses incurred through the receipt of money from shippers, e.g. pin-makers, to pay for the transportation service rendered. He would have found, of course, that such proprietors naturally turned to trying to "make money," too. They paid out money from capital funds to somehow acquire the capital items needed and to operate their firms and they would count on getting back more money for the services sold.

Indeed one of the significant advances in theory subsequent

to the 1776 publication of Smith's . . . *Wealth of Nations* is that efficient marketing is production, too, creating place and time and ownership utilities. This adds with economy of effort to the sum total of human want satisfaction. Accordingly we must go back and acknowledge as producers those merchants who began not long after the Crusades to travel from Western Europe and England to the East to purchase and bring back exotic goods for the new-found Western markets. Indeed, such functioning as merchants involved the first true division of labor (if one does not count the natural specialization of the members of a household). It is clear that each and every one who served as a merchant-middleman found it necessary to raise money somehow to use as capital funds, whether he traveled by land or by water. Obviously operation by barter became, not only cumbersome, but wholly impossible. Any and each self-respecting analyst easily can visualize for himself the several kinds of money costs and expenses such a merchant necessarily incurred even if operating as a sole proprietor.

A merchant would require even more money capital funds if or as soon as he might expand his venture and hire one or more companions as employees. And if a partnership were formed for an overland venture, the capital funds required per capita for those who thus combined to make the journey might be little changed, yet might prove even a bit more economical. If the commerce were carried on by water, almost of necessity, more capital funds would be invested in capital equipment and the scale of operations would have to be expanded to include sufficient wage-earners at least to man one ship. The wages and provisions would involve the laying out of money to cover operating expenses. In fact, by the time such trade began to become significant, the venturers entered into the business of taking goods, especially woolens, on the outbound journey, too. As these kinds of commerce grew and grew in the early modern period, in the few centuries after the

Crusades, the extent of trade is sometimes characterized as the "Commercial Revolution."

By the 1490s, customary trade routes were so badly interdicted that bold searches were undertaken to find new, alternate routes, resulting in the discovery of America and, a very few years later, the discovery of the route to India around to the south of Africa.

Concurrently, as Wesley C. Mitchell has reported, double-entry accounting was "invented" in Italy in 1494. However, it seems to me that "invented" is not the truly appropriate word for that which was done was to make adequately formal the practices that had grown to be customary. Such double-entry accounting then, as it has ever since, recorded profits (those available to distribute as dividends) only as the result of antecedent successful selling of products for more than the costs and expenses appropriately allocated to the items sold. Successful selling preceded the recording of profits and, of course, the paying of dividends. Profits realization was (and remains) a matter of *turnover of assets*. A double exchange is a fitting description. Profit is made if the money value of the assets grows, almost invariably through what money is recovered from sales above those money costs and expenses involved in producing the items. When done successfully, the liability side of the balance sheet is increased correspondingly to show that the firm (treated as a separate entity) becomes further obligated to the owners (treated as distinct entities) of the enterprise as much as the assets have grown. Obviously businessmen sellers were not in that earlier period (and are not today) paying out as much money to finance producing as they expected to recover via sales. The aggregate incomes created in connection with producing are not as much as the aggregate "value." The attempts on the parts of the merchants of western Europe in the early centuries of the modern period to "make money" in the sense of obtaining more money generally in selling goods than the money costs and expenses they had incurred out of their money capital funds in conducting their businesses can be described as wholly "natural." It was easy to conjure up. Indeed, no one ever, not up to the present day, seems to have conjured up any good alternative for those free enterprise ventures, ventures which must, to be efficient, raise significant amounts of money capital funds and must make disbursements from such funds to meet costs and expenses before there is anything ready to sell.

And that type of money-making was so natural that apparently exactly the same objective evolved independently many centuries earlier as considerable trade around the Mediterranean Sea developed in the Ancient World. It became so prominent then that Aristotle and the Greeks named it "chrematistics." Hence a systematic analysis of the money-making system evolved naturally by free enterprise aptly can be called "Chrematistical Economics." It absorbs, rounds out, and makes into a distinguishable whole the Institutional Economics of Thorstein Veblen, John R. Commons, and Wesley C. Mitchell.

In the decades between the 1490s and 1776, the leading English international merchants multiplied in numbers and their average business size grew and grew. Their business was broadened considerably by their participation in other phases of production, especially the making of woolens. They were responsible for developing the "cottage" or "putting out" system, whereby the processing and manufacturing of textiles was divided among several households. The wealthy merchants (commonly acting via their agents) supplied to diverse households, scattered along the roadways between towns, the specialized equipment and the raw material or the partly processed goods. On completion of the assigned work, the merchants paid for and carried off the output to another household for further processing. The high degree of division of labor in this system, with great repetition of standardized motions, helped to make possible and bring on the "Great Inventions" beginning in the first half of the

1700s. That, together with the perfection of the steam engine in 1760, caused the Industrial Revolution.

Both the Cottage System, *i.e.*, Putting-Out System, on the one hand and the Factory System on the other hand required businessmen and their organizations to assemble still larger sums of capital funds and to pay out costs and expenses in connection with the diverse steps in form utility creation as well as in marketing. More and more it became clear that the money paid from business capital funds was moving in a circuit flow with a circuit velocity matching that of the production time span. As a description of business the "transaction turnover" concept of circulation, long found in economic theory, was in fact outdated several centuries prior to the recognition by economists in the 1920s of money's circuit flow and circuit velocity. These latter aptly might also be called "income-creating circulation."

J.B. Say's work has been described as simply having had the purpose of making more orderly and popular what he understood Adam Smith to have said. But from the . . . *Wealth of Nations* Say had almost no grounds or justification for developing or asserting "Say's Law of Markets." Smith saw clearly that the leading merchants, the businessmen of his era, were trying to make money. Philosophically he disliked that, criticized it, condemned it, and asserted that those who were pursuing money-making ought not to do so. They ought, instead, to pursue the welfare of the people. It was the production of a large average amount of want-satisfying goods and their distribution which he regarded as the wealth of the nation. He was convinced that the pursuit of money-making, of profits, was somewhat of a road-block that stood in the way, although he acknowledged a need for a "reasonable profit." In numerous spots in his book he, while condemning the Mercantile System, noted that the businessmen of his time were buying to sell again, were buying to sell with a profit, were trying to "buy cheap" and "sell dear." However, to my mind his most striking sentence is: "The merchants and artificer . . . acted merely from a view of their own interest, and in pursuit of their own peddlar[sic] principle of turning a penny wherever a penny was to be got" (Stirling and Slade, 1819, Edinburgh, . . . *Wealth of Nations*, vol. II, p. 196). Of this last quotation, let it be emphasized that Smith included "artificers" as also striving to make money. It seems that he saw the proprietors of manufacturing ventures, including that of making pins, as having adopted the same objective, different from that of consumers generally, that had been developed by the merchants. J.B. Say, if his purpose were to better organize Smith's views and to popularize them, and also to describe existing reality, ought never to have asserted Say's Law of Markets. Businessmen neither in 1776 nor in 1803 (the date of Say's first edition) in disbursing money from their capital funds were creating buyer incomes adequate to equal the total prices they required for their products.

In the very early stages of the Commercial Revolution, when the scale of operation of the international merchants was usually small and their numbers few, their making some money by way of obtaining money selling prices that on the average exceeded the money costs and expenses they had incurred out of capital funds must have made only minor impact. But as the numbers of such ventures increased greatly through many decades and the average size of each surviving enterprise increased significantly, their success necessarily eventuated in more and more concentration in the merchants' hands of the money supply of each nation in western Europe. Since western European areas are reported to have produced virtually no gold and silver, the garnering of more and then more money as profits by the merchants of those leading commercial nations undoubtedly tended to become ever more difficult. Of course, the apparently growing "shortage" of money made increasingly difficult financial success according to the objective that naturally had been evolved. There did seem to be a shortage of money. The money incomes created through the regular business cost-and-expense payments disbursed from capital funds to finance production failed on the whole (or average) to equal the total minimum prices that were satisfactory or reasonable to the profits-pursuing businessmen. There almost always seemed then, as virtually always seems now, to be a shortage of money. Success and prosperity generally for the big merchants of England and Atlantic-European nations began, from the start of the Commercial Revolution, to appear contingent on making sure that added money would continue right along to be inserted into the circulation. Hence it was not at all surprising that soon the business leaders hit upon the idea that additional money (gold and/or silver, coined or as bullion) must be obtained from abroad, if possible from areas where new gold and silver were produced, but even if necessary from past accumulations in foreign lands. Of course it would be preferable to garner such money-metals through trade, a favorable balance. But the leaders and persons of great influence in Spain and nations north thereof were not above obtaining by other means such money or bullion from accumulations abroad, especially from less economically developed areas, sometimes taking much of these as spoils of war and of conquest.

The methods devised for assuring one's western European "home" country a favorable balance of payments included the founding of colonies by settlement of relatively unsettled lands and by subjugating the so-called "uncivilized" people already there. Colonies, whether founded by colonization or by conquest, were intended to function for the benefit of the "mother country." This meant that the former supplied cheaply to the latter raw materials and other products needed but not readily supplied "at home." It meant also that those colonies were to serve as markets, and expected to buy dearly items turned out in their "home country." In a sense the colonies were counted upon to be taken advantage of, to be exploited.

In concert, wages of the workers and "common people" in

each western European "mother country" were regulated so as to hold down unit costs of items produced for export. The fundamental objective was to assure that the more developed, trading, "mother" nation would enjoy a favorable balance of trade (better, of "payments") and would garner continuously an inflow of standard money or money metals. The resulting increase in the money supply made it possible for its businessmen, its big mercantile firms and artificer-manufacturers, to make money on the whole (or on the average) by being able to sell stock-in-trade or output for prices that exceeded the money costs and expenses properly allocated to each item being sold. "England's treasure by foreign trade" was in fact the business profits and general prosperity resulting from that inflow of acceptable money. That increase in the country's money supply, the resulting money inflow, yielded money profits.

Be it emphasized that as businessmen, the merchants and the artificers were not regulated. It was a system of "free enterprise." To be sure, big firms often reaped the benefits from export bounties (as well as from import duties). But those were intended to be aids and benefits to them rather than restrictions. "Regulated Companies" were regulated to keep prices *up*! It was the workers and the families producing on the land, the common-people-consumers at "home," who were constrained and forced to pay higher prices for products handled by merchants or processed by artificers because of the regulations and duties and navigation laws. Also it was the people in the colonies as well as in backward parts of the whole world who were victimized. Bounties, benefiting the exporter ventures, required people at "home" to pay higher taxes while the corn laws, to permit holding wages down, were burdens on families attached to the land. To be sure, merchants and artificer businessmen undoubtedly were required to pay taxes, too, but that cannot be reasoned to have involved "regulation." The building up of a nation's "strength" did occur also. It was a necessary by-product, inescapable as a means of installing and maintaining those regulations advocated by profit-pursuing business firms. "Enterprise" was essentially "free." Government "interference" was aimed basically to benefit the profits pursuers of the day.

Adam Smith saw clearly that the leading merchants and artificers on the whole were striving to make money and that the government interferences and regulations, aimed to aid them toward that objective, eventuated overall detrimentally. As we look back, we see that wage-earners and workers on the land were suppressed and their welfare flouted. We see that the people in colonies were counted upon to be victimized by being restrained from producing some items at costs that would have improved their living standards. Also they were virtually forced to sell their exports at cheap prices and buy other items, especially manufactured goods, at prices relatively too high. And we can see that numerous wars were fought as a result of the mercantilistic drive of western European governments to coddle their business-men both by pushing to colonize less-developed areas of the world and to take as spoils from more "backward" people their accumulations of precious metals. We can see also that many other wars resulted; wars between empires, with nations ambi-tious to become empires, and wars of rebellion, both rebellions of colonies and internally (as in America and in France). Smith was justified in being critical of Mercantilism and condemning it. But he simply did not comprehend that it was an altogether natural evolution stemming from his beloved division of labor. Such a division inevitably requires that money be used as capital funds since production, including marketing, must as a result involve a time-consuming flow, a series of steps becoming so numerous that money costs and expenses paid out of capital funds must take on counter income circulation with a circular velocity that matches the pace of the flow of output. Since he did nothing to comprehend or explain the naturally resulting money-making objective, he suggested no alternative or useful alteration and supplied no insights that help us devise anything to install in place of what the great merchants followed by the artificers were taking as their goal. If the essence of the Mercantile System is the objective of business enterprise to make money by succeeding in selling stock-in-trade or output at prices higher than costs and expenses incurred in production (the marketing as well as the making), then that System has lived on, contrary to Adam Smith's recommendation.

There is a belief, likely a mistaken idea when fully evaluated among economists and historians, that Mercantilism virtually ceased to exist after around 1800. The following is a quotation from a highly regarded volume of general reference: "It was modified and largely superceded by the economic system of the physiocrates and the system of laissez-faire." It is true that many of the regulations were "superceded" (even including some reduction, but seldom elimination, of import duties). But the essence of the Mercantile System, undoubtedly the pursuit of money-making as the principal objective of business enterprises, remains. That basic money-making objective, instead of being displaced by around 1800, has spread and spread. Its fundamental importance has come to control the vast majority of production efforts and the employers of most of the workers in the U.S. and in other leading business nations. However, there is a vast number of free enterprise ventures each so relatively very, very small that their owners could be reconciled to remain in operation even if they pay themselves only wages as workers and/or salaries as managers. By the ninth decade of the twentieth century here in the U.S.A., less than three percent (3%) of our ventures large enough to take in an annual revenue of $1,000,000 each together employ fully 75% to 80% all employed workers. They carry out a similar portion of the whole of production (as measured by revenue). As a result of the Great Inventions, starting in England in the first half of the

1700s, the appearance of firms that required much capital funds out of which to meet costs and expenses has spread to huge factories, and in time to railroads and later to other kinds of transportation, to communication and electronics, to supplying power, to entertainment (including radio and television), to construction, to food processing, to the making and using of computers and office machines, to the extraction of minerals, and even of late to some aspects of agricultural production. And of course merchants and ship owners have grown bigger and bigger. The leading firms in nearly every one of those and other kinds of production have come to pursue money profit-making as their principal or first goal, along with the descendants of the mercantilists who evolved it. Note that the attention above is to "producers" (those firms striving to make money simply by handling money or manipulating finance or by speculating are ignored), and the big firms among such producers let money-making take precedence over producing. That primary goal evolved by the mercantilists simply has grown more pervasive and more dominant these last two centuries. Since accepted, customary double-entry accounting on the one hand and corporate law on the other preclude any profits distribution out of capital funds but require profit to be earned and recorded antecedently; all such big firms, collectively dominant, in the course of their producing create incomes for potential buyers of output that are insufficient to equal the aggregate value of that output. The shortfall is the amount of profit they require.

But whereas the nature of the mercantilistic objective, that of making money, a reasonable money profit, via a firm's selling at money prices more than its money costs and expenses, remains and has spread and grown stronger and far more pervasive, the principal method by which to attain that goal for business as a whole (or on the average) changed drastically and fundamentally during the 1700s. And that new process or method of generating widespread profits is far more subtle than formerly. Prior to about

1700, the sole method during several centuries for assuring that free enterprise firms in any business nation of western Europe would be able to realize reasonable money profits and that prosperity would prevail generally was to decree regulations, under sovereign authority, to make sure that there be virtually continuously a favorable balance of trade (payments). Such regulations were aimed to assure an inflow of acceptable money or money metals. Regulations "at home," such as those to hold down wages and price of "corn," plus import duties and export bounties and other regulations applicable abroad, especially in colonies a "mother" nation could establish or conquer, were all directed to that money-inflow end. But after 1700 the method of assuring "success" and prosperity to large and leading business ventures that pursued the goal of money profits turned rapidly to the reliance more and more upon the commercial banks increasing the volume of money in circulation via their creation of additional new money, via their "monetizing" more and more debts of borrowers to whom loans are made. As the outstanding total of such bank loans is increased, the borrowers do, of course, insert the added money into the circulation in one way or another. As such new commercial banking got going in the 1700s, and fully by 1800, the need to rely on favorable balances of trade (or payments) declined and there was less and less needed to maintain former onerous regulation at "home" or in the colonies that characterized a long period prior to 1700.

"Commercial banks" that create added new money by "monetizing debts," by transforming the debts of borrowers into what serves effectively as money (now in the U.S., Federal Reserve Notes out in circulation plus bank demand deposits subject to checks) were administered "the spark of life" by the unlikely and apparently innocuous event known as the "Forced Loan of 1640." The "Forced Loan" described the act of the then English king's having "borrowed" one night, without asking permission, the funds that London businessmen (actually big merchants) had become accustomed to leaving for safe-keeping overnight in the Tower of London. Soon after the Forced Loan, those merchants began to leave their funds, instead, with diverse of the goldsmiths in and around Lombard Street. Although several other types of "banking" antedated the resulting "commercial banking," some by many centuries, it was the leaving of considerable sums of money in the hands of private contractors, in this case goldsmiths owning strongboxes and employing nightwatchmen, for *safekeeping* that evolved into money-creating operation by such depositories.

Instead of a merchant's simply depositing his funds over-night and over non-business periods, some of them soon developed the habit of leaving, nearly continuously, large portions of their cash in such deposits. They could make payments by transferring to payees either some goldsmith's receipts or, if deposits and withdrawals were entered in a deposit book, by payment by one's goldsmith according to correctly drawn and signed "negotiable orders of withdrawal" to named payees. Since those payees often already were patronizing the same or another goldsmith (or would elect to inaugurate such an arrangement), the lawful money stayed almost in whole in the hands of goldsmiths, even though a minor but changing amount tended to flow around among those goldsmith-bankers to settle clearing balances. Accordingly the lawful money initially left for safekeeping seemed mostly to lie idle and unused, even while title to it was being transferred, generally by circulating goldsmith receipts or by checks of merchants and artificers who had contracted with diverse of the London goldsmiths. That seemingly idle money apparently could be lent to others. However, as loans began to be made, haltingly at first, it soon was found that borrowers generally preferred to become depositors also (if not already patronizing one of the goldsmiths). Hence the making of loans caused only a minor decrease in the "lawful money" on deposit with the goldsmiths, collectively considered. More, and then still more, loans were found possible and most of the the lawful money began to serve essentially as reserves. So it eventuated that the total of loans made could bulk to several times the amount of lawful-money-reserves, possibly even as much as ten times, before the lenders or the depositors began to feel unsafe and somewhat doubtful about the ability of the goldsmith-bankers to redeem their receipts and/or their deposits in full-embodied or lawful money. Note that such a goldsmith-banker, willing to make more and more loans because of holding adequate "idle" reserves, by one single stroke built up both his "assets" (usually called "resources" by bankers) by his acquiring some sort of interest-bearing promise(s) to pay from the borrower, and equally built up his liabilities either in the form of the outstanding bank notes he issued (now of greatly curtailed use except by central bankers because of regulations that were evolved to prevent excess) or (mainly now) demand deposits subject to transfer or withdrawal by the use of checks.

In negotiating commercial bank loans, borrowers go into debt. The opposite side of debt is the concept of "credit." It is worth repeating: When commercial banks make loans and thus extend credit, borrowers go into debt. Note also that when money is saved by some income recipients and such savings are lent to others, credit is extended also by those lenders and debt is incurred by the borrowers. The result is that with the development of commercial banks, there came into existence a second source of loanable funds and two kinds of credit. There is "saved credit" involved in the lending of savings, and on the other hand there is "non-saved credit" involved in the operation of commercial banking when loans are extended that increase the money supply. When a commercial bank uses the techniques evolved by the goldsmiths to make loans there is no equivalent prior saving. The "credit instrument" resulting is a promise by the borrower to repay a specified sum of money, which bank "asset" is matched simply by an increased liability of the bank as the amount of added bank notes it has issued is increased or as its demand deposits are enlarged. Recognition of the distinction between "saved" credit and "non-saved" credit is of great importance for an analyst's clear thinking. "Thrift institutions" historically have confined their operations to dealing in the former. But in recent years, some of them have invaded the other preserve. Conversely, "commercial banks" historically have concentrated largely on the non-saved credit types of operations, but in recent years have invaded more and more the preserve of the thrift institutions. There now is much mixing and blurring.

Incidentally, there is another type of "non-saved credit," namely, "open-book credit," including charge accounts which often but not always can be extended in a way to enable their outstanding total to be enlarged without there being resort to any prior money savings. To illustrate, consider the whole of retailers as a group and assume that the total of retail sales absorb entirely the whole of the incomes of consumers that have been created by the financing by business of producing and marketing. Retailers collectively can sell the whole of their stock-in-trade for a few percent more than costs and expenses simply by setting their prices a bit above all costs and then extending added, undiscounted, open-book credit equal in total to the margin of profit they attain. As those retailers will have recovered in cash, via consumers having spent the whole of their money incomes, enough to continue functioning, that open-book credit simply will serve to the extent that its outstanding total grows to enlarge the retailers' assets and will be matched by an equal amount of increase on the other side of their balance sheets via enlargement of the item of "profits" or "net earnings." Instead of there being an equivalent amount of prior savings that is lent when such credit is extended and enlarged, it turns out that the source of such added credit is that self-same profit to which the credit extension gives birth.

Another insight which seems to me to be essential to

comprehend adequately our financial system and its functioning is the distinction between "price inflation" and what it is my preference to call "debt-inflation" or "financial inflations." We can experience considerable, even great, debt-inflation while experiencing little or no general price increases. The reverse relationship theoretically is quite possible although much less common. The last period, prior to recent years in which significant debt-inflation took place in the U.S. even while prices on the whole remained essentially unchanged, was 1923 to 1929, and much the same can be said for the several years between 1873 and 1890. In both time spans our industrial output was growing at a rapid rate and unit costs were shrinking as fast or even a bit faster than the rate at which the nation's money supply was increasing as the result in the main of our commercial banks creating added money through a net enlargement of the debts of borrowers, debts which were being monetized.

At the present time, this ninth decade of the twentieth century, the attention of nearly everyone seems again to be focused fiercely on the swelling of debts, especially of those debts that are being monetized. It is the burden of debts connected to the expansion of non-saved credit that is in fact the great threat to the survival of our financial system and to our system of free enterprise. In the last year or so, mid-1980s, our money supply has been ballooning at the rate of more than 11% per annum, almost in whole by increase in commercial-bank-created money, including enlargement of Federal Reserve notes as our banking system transforms more and more debts into money. Now, as all up-to-date economists will know, many groups have fallen very deeply into debt, debt on which the interest as well as repayment of principal are for many very great burdens. Groups included in what now may be called "big debtors" are: a) consumers whose installment debts have grown more than 20% per annum these last two or three years, b) farmers, c) petroleum wildcatters and others in the recently expanded petroleum service firms, d) Latin

American governments and some of their nationals plus similar borrowers in other partly developed portions of this world, e) "take-over" organizations or "artists," f) builders on their "construction loans," and g) the U.S. federal government. A great portion, but not all of these foregoing debts, has been financed by commercial bank credit expansion, the process which creates added money to the extent there be net increase in the amount outstanding as new extensions exceed those debts concurrently paid off. For example, over several decades the increase in outstanding installment credit has involved about 50% "non-saved" commercial bank credit. (Note that home mortgage loans have not been included since they continue to be funded mainly out of "saved credit").

In 1776, when Smith's . . . *Wealth of Nations* was first published, and even in 1803 at the time of publication of Say's initial work, it is likely that a huge number of little free enterprise ventures carried on at least 75% of all production, the marketing as well as the form utility creation, possibly as much as 90%, and that the very few big merchants and artificers were responsible for only the remaining minor amount. Perhaps those many, many little ventures could be regarded as supplying to potential buyers of end products sufficient total purchasing power as the result of the money disbursements they made, since wages as workers and salaries as managers for such little entrepreneurs may have been adequate rewards so that no true "net profit" was required to keep them operating. Laissez faire might have applied fully for them, yet clearly not for the few large merchants and artificers. But now in the ninth decade of the 1900s, a very few big firms, only 2% to 3% of all enterprises, employing fully 75% of our workers who have jobs, carry out at least 75% of the production, the creation of time and place and ownership utilities as well as form utilities. They are big in order to take full advantage of the benefits of division of labor and of the economies of scale. Little firms cannot compete and survive. The former dominate, overwhelmingly.

In order to succeed and to be willing or able to continue operations they must realize net profit by selling at money prices which exceed at least by some few percent those money costs they have paid out from their capital funds, which latter almost always have had to be raised from "absentee owners." Otherwise they are precluded from distributing any profits-dividends to those equity owners.

Prior to about 1700, big merchant (and artificer) firms in western Europe for several centuries had relied upon favorable balances of trade to bring in added acceptable money. The added money would, on the whole, enable them to sell, at home and abroad, for more money than their money costs. However, the commercial banking processes began around 1700 to supply more and more money that those new type lenders created by monetizing debts. And since political and philosophical and military revolutions, at home and abroad, especially in colonies, curtailed many of the mercantilistic regulations by 1800, the result was that reliance came to be placed more and more on the expansion of non-saved credit, the monetizing of debts, by the goldsmith-evolved commercial banks. These new-type banks became the means of increasing the money supply and, for the time being, increasing buyer purchasing power beyond those incomes yielded merely from the financing of production.

It may help if the reader visualize the working of such expansion of non-saved credit by commercial banking. Consider a big firm that employs many thousands of workers and assume that such organization typifies all of the big firms which together now do fully 75% of all producing. Such a firm must have raised a large sum of money capital, mainly from absentee owners. Its highly subdivided labor and resulting economies of scale make its unit costs far below the unit costs of any small producer who might try to turn out virtually identical items. It really competes only with a few other large firms, each of which is organized in almost precisely the same way. As it pays out money to meet its production costs and expenses, it creates, sooner or later by way of the circular flow, incomes for potential buyers of end products. Being almost invariably a corporation, corporate law as well as approved accounting precludes it from paying dividends (purportedly from profits) until adequate profits previously have been earned and recorded. For it, "normal price" for a unit of output likely is equal to the properly allocated costs and expenses of that item *plus* that percentage of markup that to it, as a seller, seems at least to be reasonable. But if it is not the most efficient producer with whom it does in fact compete in its line, its "normal price" instead likely will be lower, *i.e.*, the allocated costs and expenses plus satisfactory margin of markup of that most efficient, competing producer. Clearly, the workers will not receive as wages sufficient money incomes to buy and pay in full for their share of the output. The margin of markup in general measures the shortfall for the firm's workers (as it does also for other participants, such as farmers who supply raw materials). But if some of the workers, in addition to having spent their entire incomes (some perhaps indirectly via savings to help buy newly produced capital goods), can be induced to promise to pay some more in the future, perhaps by contracting some installment debts, collectively they can meet the prices demanded by the sellers even while acquiring the whole share of the output intended for them. About half of the rising installment debt historically has been financed by the extension and enlargement of the non-saved credit of commercial banks that create the added money they lend. Indubitably by acquiring added newly created "bank money" and spending that along with their wage incomes, they, as buyers, can pay to sellers more than the latters' cost and expenses. The same is true of other buyers, such as farmers, who otherwise participate in production and then become consumers, too. As long as there continues to be enlargement of money injected somewhere around the circle of financing producing, since the circuit flow has a circuit velocity corresponding to that of the average production span, buyers apparently are able to pay big-business sellers more than the latter's unit costs and expenses. Business firms for the time being thus will realize money profits of the type they pursue.

Further, if money profits once realized from the spending of new non-saved credit money always were distributed as dividends by the recipient firms and always then simply spent for end-products, the "new money" injections in an initial production period seemingly could go on and on to eventuate in an equal profit in the next average production period and similarly in subsequent periods. However, two kinds of actions tend to prevent that. On the one hand, profitable firms usually "plow back in" some of their profits so that total production costs and expenses naturally rise a bit in each succeeding production span, although price per unit may not rise if efficiency increases and output is expanded. On the other hand the consumer-buyers, such as workers and farmers, may press strongly, even violently as by strikes, to obtain higher wage rates and higher farm prices in the hopes of buying their shares of the subsequent output (often urged upon them by high-pressure means) and also to pay off and get free of past debt. Accordingly, it really takes further new injections of money, created out of non-saved credit, to keep the realization of profits steady on the average for big production firms, through span after production span. These things turn out to work as a great pump, as also does the expansion of bank-credit money from injection elsewhere. Similar to the Labor-Union-Wage-Increase Pump that through production cycle after production cycle keeps puffing up our debt-inflation (as long as some sort of limit is not reached to our monetizing debt) are the Agricultural-Output-and-Subsidies Pump, the Indexation Pump, the Foreign-Aid Pump, the Borrowing-Against-Rising-Capital-Values Pump, the Take-Over-and/or-Recapitalization Pump, and many of these are connected with the almost perpetual Government-Deficit Pump.

To speed this summary for economists, let me assert that there is no justification for any puzzlement about the cause and nature of what is known as "business cycles," but which might better be labeled "business financial spasms." Prosperity is brought on simply by the expansion and injection of new money into money's circuit flow, moving counter to the flow of output at the same velocity as the latter. It is an inevitable result of the banking operation of monetizing more and more non-saved credit. Such money expansion is followed by a pause when some sort of limit is approached or reached, and that sometimes is followed by actions to liquidate some (or many) of the debts that have been created. Big business on the one hand tends to be able to sell for more than costs and expenses as long as money increase is swinging along merrily. We are said to enjoy prosperity. But as we pause in the monetizing of more and more non-saved credit, profits on the whole shrink and tend after a while (but not at once, since that portion of past profits that are distributed as dividends and then devoted exclusively to spending for consumption will repeat the yielding of profits again) to average zero so that we experience "recession." Some recessions culminate in efforts to liquidate some or many of the debts. A net paying off of debts that reduces non-saved credit outstanding extinguishes money and is the converse side of the expansion and monetization of such credit. Thereupon we truly suffer "depression." In depression, if significant liquidation of such earlier debts occurs and reduces outstanding non-saved credit, on the average current output cannot be sold even for as much as costs. Moreover, if current output is sold without loss, debts cannot be paid off net.

Wesley C. Mitchell reported that investigations at the National Bureau of Economic Research ascertained that the first catastrophe that was truly a depression (symbolized by much starvation because there seems to be offered too much of most all kinds of goods including food, which cannot be sold, *i.e.*, bought at satisfactory prices) took place in the 1720s. Recall that money-creating commercial banking was administered the spark of life by the Forced Loan of 1640. Afterwards various goldsmiths were engaged by London merchants to hold for safekeeping some of the former's money funds. The latter, before long, discovered that they could lend out such "idle" money, not once but several times. Many goldsmiths became commercial bankers, and during the second decade of the 1700s John Law gained permission of the government of France to float a bank of the newly developed commercial type to assume and fund a large part of the French national debt and to help finance and run the commerce with the Mississippi country. That Mississippi Bubble burst with highly disturbing repercussions in the early 1720s. Meanwhile a similar scheme was undertaken in England by the South Sea Company (incorporated in 1711). The bank created therein was to assume and extinguish much of the English national debt in exchange for a monopoly privilege on the trade with the South Sea. In 1720, the year then called "The South Sea Year," it proposed to buy the whole national debt. That South Sea Bubble also burst in the early 1720s; fraud sometimes is alleged to have been involved in working up that English bubble. Furthermore those two pricked-balloon outcomes just as validly can be regarded as the first financial business depression of the free enterprise system.

So long as we keep monetizing more and more debts (more non-saved credit being extended than that which concurrently is paid off and extinguished), buyers are able to purchase the output of producing firms at prices which exceed what those firms have incurred as actual money costs and expenses per unit. That is supplemented usually by the increase also of accumulated inventory and outstanding, undiscounted open-book credit. The average business makes money and enjoys prosperity, total profits likely being greater than the current expansions, since added circulating money likely yields similar though dwindling effects through subsequent production periods.

However, those financial expansions always have been punctuated by pauses from time to time, and at greater intervals reach a climax and come to an end. The underlying cause of cessation of such financial expansion more often than not has tended to be some limit on the amount of new money the commercial banks are able to create and put into circulation as, for example, the legal requirement that there be held as reserves a minimum percentage of gold behind bank demand deposits and/or bank notes. But this may be affected, especially the timing, by a great variety of other factors, such as apprehension that too much debt is being incurred, or that too much credit has been extended, or that a major crop has failed, or that inventory has become top-heavy, or that a big bank has failed due to fraud or mere ineptness, or that there is a political upheaval at home or abroad, or that a military conflict breaks out somewhere, etc. If a nation has completely abandoned any tie between precious metals and the creation of "bank money" (as now here in the U.S. since the mid-1960s and early 1970s), the creation and injection of new money ("managed money") created by commercial banks might run on and on until its value declines and further declines until eventually it has to be "devalued" or even becomes worthless.

Depression takes place when and if we try to liquidate and markedly reduce the great accumulation of debts. Such debts will have to be paid, to whatever extent paid, out of current incomes, or instead current product (if all be sold) will have to be sold at significant loss. Otherwise if current product does move to buyers even in exchange for prices which recover for sellers no more on average than costs and expenses (devoid of any true profit), the built-up burden of debt cannot be liquidated. It will result in default instead. Depression is a *financial* debacle. My prediction is that we shall experience by far our biggest depression relatively soon, sometime in the next few years, say no later than the year 2000. Since we in the U.S. now use "managed" irredeemable money without any except man-decreed reserve requirements, our commercial banking operations are running along creating new money at a rapid rate. Recently that rate was at about 11% per year compound (if the available statistical data is reliable). Such a rate will double our money supply in about 6-1/2 years. Can free enterprise survive until the turn of the century if, by monetizing more and more debts, we blow up our money supply by then to more than four times its size now in the mid-1980s? And if we cease that expansion, what happens to our (and Japan and Hong Kong and Western Europe and OPEC) "prosperity"?

There is another realization which already may have come to the mind of any truly astute reader, namely, that the foregoing description of the cause of business financial spasms or "business cycles" is inevitably valid even regardless of whether or not the financing of production of itself naturally does create incomes in aggregate equal to the total value of the output. Even if "demand-sider" Keynes' proposition which he declares to be indubitable, were valid so that

> ". . . the incomes derived in the aggregate by all the elements in the community concerned in a productive activity necessarily has a value exactly to the *value* of the output."

and if the essential premise underlying *Say's Law of Markets* always were true and if the assertions by George Gilder, spokesman for the "supply-siders," were invariably valid, expansions and contractions of "artificial financial mechanisms" would cause free enterprise as we know it to enjoy added prosperities, and then of course it would suffer depressions, neither of which have any predetermined periodicity nor amplitude. Even if each big capitalistic firm actually were to pay out from its capital funds as among or along with its costs and expenses a minimum amount of profit on that same item of output (as Gilder mistakenly has reasoned, contrary to the restraints of both accounting and corporation law), the expansion of added, newly created, non-saved bank-credit-money would enable buyers of end products to pay *even more* in purchasing the output. The holding back of a portion, although small, of the output by producers while they sell the rest would enable buyers to pay *more* than unit costs and expenses for that major fraction of output which those purchasers do acquire. Similarly, even if the whole output is sold, if the sellers extend and the buyers undertake more and more undiscounted open-book credit in purchasing that whole output, the total money which is paid and agreed to be paid by buyers in the future will exceed the costs and expenses of what is sold. As long as these three "artificial financial mechanisms" continue to expand and the total of them outstanding grows bigger and bigger, sellers necessarily will record *more* profit than possible had such expansions not taken place. However, after a lapse of time, each of the expansions and accumulations tends to become top-heavy. If our money-creating banks (as historically when U.S. bank reserve requirements included precious metals) continue making more and more loans until those outstanding approach the limit their reserve requirements will permit, causing further lending to slow down, even to cease, and eventually lead to nothing more than curtailment of their lending, the profits realized on continued output will decline. If there are strong and successful efforts to collect, reducing the bank money outstanding in circulation, that itself will leave potential buyers with less to spend on current products. Further, average selling prices will be reduced below current costs and expenses. If there is strong determination to force onto the market, sell off, and thus reduce some of the accumulated inventory (which is especially likely, since unit prices are declining), that will leave potential buyers in possession of still less to spend on current output. If there is success in collecting (*i.e.*, debtors paying off) some of the total of outstanding open-book credit, that will reduce still further the money from current incomes left in the hands of potential buyers with which to purchase currently produced goods. To the extent that there is accomplished reduction in the bank-credit money that had been extended and in the inventory that had been accumulated (accumulated actually without need for any prior saving of money) and in the amount of undiscounted open-book credit which has been extended without need for financing via any prior money savings, current output can be disposed of only at prices which on the average will result in significant money losses. The building up and accumulating of more and more of these "artificial financial mechanisms" naturally will enlarge the showing or recording of heightened business profits, hence will yield more propserity. And the curtailment and then liquidation of accumulations of those "artificial financial mechanisms" naturally culminates in the recording of losses for capitalistic firms that have raised funds mainly from absentee owners, hence will cause depression. There usually are pauses between prosperity and depression, generally called "recession" and "recovery."

Business financial spasms (nee business cycles) are caused mainly by periods of non-saved-credit debt-inflation yielding general business profits, each such period followed by one of debt-deflation yielding general business losses.

Focus briefly on another aspect of the now dominant money-making, *i.e.*, chrematistics, that has come to overpower and control in fact want-satisfying economics, namely, its highly disturbing and threatening international aspects. Comments here will be extremely brief, but importance is of transcendent magnitude. For one who desires to obtain a full sense of what lies ahead in the relationships between the highly developed business nations and the less developed portions of the "free world" it is recommended that he read carefully Chapter 9. From that mere first approximation he will obtain, it seems to me, a clear vision of the fatal difficulty that so-called "free enterprise," if unchanged, undoubtedly will drown in.

All reasonably well-prepared economists and historians will know already the great conflicts and difficulties brought on "at home" in leading European nations as well as in the more "backward" parts of the world as results of the pervasive regulations and military adventures that eventuated from the Mercantile System when it relied upon a "favorable balance of trade" as the device for bringing in acceptable money or money metals in order to provide profitability and prosperity for artificers and the big merchants, sometimes called "Merchant Princes." The severe treatment and suppressive regulations saddled on the natives and the colonists in the less-developed areas and on the wage-workers and serfs and peasants in western Europe eventually culminated in rebellion or revolution, as in the American Revolution and the French Revolution.

Now, in the late 1980s, the situation in the "Third World" countries (brought on by Modern Mercantilism) is as bleak as it ever was in the centuries preceding Adam Smith and the revolutions mentioned. The business financial objective remains the same, that of making money, as it was for several centuries prior to 1800. But the principal method has changed and the outcome before many years promises to be equally bad, if not even far worse. Profit-pursuing business, now expanded far beyond the mere inclusion of big merchants and some artificers as mentioned by Smith, has come to rely upon buyers somewhere sinking deeper and deeper into debt, with much of the debt being monetized, as the means by which sellers are enabled to "buy cheap and sell dear." In the last twenty years, since the U.S. has set the bad example of having removed all requirements of any percentage of precious metal reserve behind "bank money" (in the U.S. "bank money" being Federal Reserve Notes in circulation as well as the demand deposits of commercial banks), we in the leading industrial and financial nations have rushed along extending more and more and still more credit, largely non-saved, commercial bank credit, to governments and other buyers in less developed lands. So long as we rush along at high speed extending even more such credit to, say, our Latin-American trading partners, we can sell dearly to them while buying relatively cheaply the materials they supply us, and we can sell more to them than we buy from them. Our business firms can make money and, hence, prosper. Moreover, if prices on the whole rise at the rate of several percent, interest cost can seem quite burdenless and rising capital values will seem to support more and still more debt, justifying increased borrowing and lending. But in time the debt-inflation likely will slow down and even come to a halt. Inflation, both price inflation and debt inflation, may slow or even stop. Inflation may run away, or go through the roof, and money may become relatively valueless or require devaluation. Banks may reach a limit on their lending power, and lenders may become apprehensive. Borrowers may become unwilling to undertake more debt, especially if price-inflation declines so as to make interest payments and principal repayment installments seem burdensome. If debtors are called upon to make interest payments plus net principal installment payments, the "house-of-cards," earlier built for firms in the highly developed nations as their prior trading prosperity and in the "developing" areas as their recently improved standard of living, will begin to topple. Somebody is going to get hurt financially. If the debtors don't make payments on schedule, the lenders (especially our commercial bankers) sometimes will be forced to suffer losses. If the debtors do continue to pay on schedule, trade will be violently dislocated. Payments, if net, not simply rescheduled into enlarged principal, likely will be possible only by increasing the existing austerity on the parts of citizens in the debtor nations, which means magnified sacrifice on the parts of those in the lower economic classes. This in time often means rebellion of which some elected political leaders in such areas recently have stated to be feared. Alternatively the debts really will not be paid. Either way, we (the U.S.A.) may try to send in our military. There is a considerable likelihood that we may drive "Third World" countries to embrace communism.

However, in America and in nations of western Europe we, too, are in danger of embracing communism if we are engulfed in another, even greater, depression as the result of failing soon to perfect the diagnosis of the congenital defect of our big-business, free enterprise system that pursues as its principal goal the making of money through using processes that heretofore we have not understood.

The final chapter, Chapter 10, of the text that follows is titled: "We, the U.S.A. and the U.S.S.R., Can Develop Our Friendship and Together Can Forestall Armageddon."

Each of our two divergent systems has serious flaws. Those flaws inherent in our big-business free enterprise system that keeps pursuing the money-making objective as its most important and controlling aim may be more serious than those of communism. Indeed it is my belief that, if we fail to develop the relevant diagnosis and therefrom devise and activate the indicated treatments for the system we call "Western democracy," it soon will succumb from its own congenital defects. It is my belief that it is within our power, if we are thoroughly analytical of all of the relevant facts, and if we are objective in pursuing our investigations and open-minded in devising the required changes, to preserve the fundamentals of a somewhat changed free enterprise system. The system now embraced by the U.S.S.R. is also burdened with some serious defects, it seems clear to me. Sincere attempts should be made by those of us in each of our two nations to find the defects and then strive with vigor and sincerity to make the improvements indicated by the correct diagnosis. We should help each other, with specifics but not with general condemnations. There is great probability that our two systems will be much more nearly alike when we have made the essential self-improvements. Each undoubtedly will be more satisfactory for a greater portion of its citizens.

Chapter 10 does offer some ideas for correct and needed changes. Those suggestions are, however, only food for capable and sincere brainstorming sessions regarding some possible beneficial minor surgery to help perpetuate the best features of our free enterprise system and also some suggestions for improving the operation of the U.S.S.R. system of communism. Please consult that chapter. The suggestions offered there are not "iron-clad." They must be viewed only as stimulants and points of departure for brainstorming sessions that should be well-organized and composed of capable and sincere participants.

CHAPTER 9

Our Big Money-Making Producing Firms Naturally Set the Stage for Rebellion in Less Developed Areas

But Japan (and some Others) May Be Reducing the United States to Colonial Status

(Note regarding this chapter: If length were to be regarded as the measure of its importance, this would be an extremely long chapter, for it is of immeasurable concern to us in the United States and of even greater concern to the sovereign states south of us in this Western Hemisphere. For several reasons the views and insights herein are sketched as briefly as possible. One justification for such curtailed treatment is that, since debt-inflation already has been enlarged so excessively and the resulting financial catastrophe seems so imminent, we surely must hasten as fast as possible to perfect the applicable diagnosis and then speedily devise and install the indicated changes, those improvements that can forestall the dire results that otherwise surely will overtake us. Further, in many respects this chapter is a plea for help, help from those who are good analysts and also thoroughly objective as well as innovative and possessed of sufficient knowledge of the history and languages of our neighbors to the south of us. Such aid is solicited and will be welcomed with sincerity).

It is a pleasure to begin this chapter by expressing great gratitude to the INSTITUTE OF THE AMERICAS, a separately endowed organization functioning as an adjunct to the University of California at San Diego, and "dedicated to the furtherances of understanding, communication and cooperation between all nations of the Americas" and development of empathy of our peoples with each other. At the inauguration ceremonies of the INSTITUTE on November 19, 1984, Carlos Andres Perez, former President of Venezuela, was the principal speaker. He was followed at the luncheon by Dr. Raul Prebisch, economist from Argentina, as the guest speaker. In each of those addresses there ran a strong note of accusation that the financial and economic troubles of the native countries of those two men and of much of the rest of Latin America are to be blamed largely on the United States and on the actions of the U.S. government and of U.S. business firms. As a consequence of the views there expressed, it became clear to me that our neighbors below our U.S. southern border are being especially victimized by the functioning of our profits-pursuing business system. We are urgently in need of more valid insights in these matters than have been developed heretofore. And we in this leading "free enterprise" capitalistic area must find the right ways to alter our practices if we are to hope to be able to forestall further extremely serious financial and economic troubles and recurrent rebellion in those nonindustrialized, financially secondary sovereign states. Those two November 19, 1984, addresses have caused me to broaden my analysis of the chrematistic system and hasten this presentation with as much speed as possible. Before, over several decades, my attention had been concentrated on investigating and explaining money-making as viewed mostly in its domestic aspects, even though some incidental consideration was devoted to some international implications. But the broadening of my work, stimulated by the two addresses at the INSTITUTE's inauguration, has opened the gate to a virtual flood of added insights of great importance. As a consequence, we should be able to perfect the required diagnoses and speedily devise and carry out those resulting prescribed changes needed to enable the best features of free enterprise to survive and enjoy improved health. If we are successful in this endeavor undoubtedly the whole of Latin America will join in my expression of gratitude to the INSTITUTE OF THE AMERICAS.

All careful scholars of the history of western Europe since the Crusades know, of course, that in what can be called the Classical Period of Mercantilism, from about 1492 to 1776, the great drive of the government in each of the leading European nations usually was to regulate financial and economic activities, both at home and abroad and particularly in its colonies, so as to create a favorable balance of trade (read payments). Some recent historians seem to believe that the principal beneficiary was intended to be the sovereign, the king and his officers and henchmen, to increase his power and that of his kingdom. But the probability is that the main beneficiaries were the great merchants for whom an inflow of acceptable money (e.g. standard money metals) would make sure that they could sell their wares for more money than they had laid out as costs and expenses, hence to realize money profits. After all, the king could not gain in any sense directly from a net inflow of acceptable money, but only through subsequent taxing. He could levy and collect taxes, as needed, even without any favorable balance of trade. However, the merchants realized their primary objective directly and at once through such a favorable balance. This latter view is the one that makes sense. And it seems in accord with the comments of Adam Smith. However, the king could gain in due course as he aided the merchants and was championed by them. They somewhat willingly could pay added taxes out of the net money profits they realized.

During that Classical Period of Mercantilism, it is reported that there were many detailed regulations of economic and financial activities. Yet a careful evaluation of those seems to show that few were burdensome to "home" business, as business. Mercantilistic regulations really were devised in large part to aid money-making enterprises, merchants largely, to realize their objective. Some controls were to help hold down the costs of production of, say, textiles made initially by handicraftsmen and later by cottagers in the "putting out" system, by keeping wages low. Some were to subsidize exports and restrict imports. Some were to compel people abroad, especially in colonies (acquired either by conquest or by settlement) to concentrate on supplying needed materials and to do so cheaply, while buying manufactured goods from sellers in the "mother" countries and do so dearly. In any case all agree that the overriding aim was to bring acceptable money or money metals into those leading mercantilistic nations of western Europe. These regulations which promised to accomplish this, plus not infrequent military action, were used to this end. Merchants profited and the sovereigns of western Europe grew strong as a by-product.

Further, history is very clear that those who were regulated in the drive to assure a continuous money flow into leading western European nations felt grievously burdened. Oppressed were both non-business citizens of "mother" nations and the residents of their colonies as well as people in less-developed areas that managed to remain independent. Diverse colonial wars were fought. Empires struck at each other. Eventually revolution took place, as in North America and in France.

However, after around 1776 (or 1800), while the mercantilistic objective remained unaltered and even spread vigorously as the result of the Industrial Revolution, the basic method employed to attain that money-making objective changed markedly. We may label these last two centuries during which capitalism has relied upon the expansion of non-saved credit as the "Bank Credit" period of mercantilism. Within our leading, most "developed" free enterprise nations we ceased relying so heavily on internal regulations and came gradually to depend upon placing more newly created purchasing power in the hand of potential buyers of end products by lending more and more bank-money. It turned out that it really made little difference to what group commercial bank loans were made, since the circular flow against the movement of products would augment the total amount that buyers of end-products could "spend," thereby permitting sellers on the whole to record money profits. Prosperity was fostered as long as the expansion of such money was continued. However, depression naturally set in when such expansion ceased and, instead, the attempt began to liquidate that prior debt-inflation.

However, it appears to me that money-creating commercial banking did not greatly affect the trade between the most developed nations and the not-so-fully developed areas until during and following World War II. It really did not reach the level of vital importance until after the mid-1960s and early 1970s when the last vestiges of any requirement that gold (and/or silver) be included as a part of the reserves behind United States bank-money were removed. In these last two decades several of our U.S. commercial banks as well as some in western Europe (and even perhaps a few in Japan and Singapore and Hong Kong) have grown huge and have engaged increasingly in international transactions. In these most recent four decades and especially in the last twenty years, they have made loans to governments and firms and individuals in less-developed nations that total the equivalent of many hundreds of billions of dollars.

Indeed the 1970s were blessed (or plagued) by a conjunction of situations and events that virtually seduced participants into great lending and borrowing, both domestically and abroad. The quantum increase in the price of petroleum, brought on by united action particularly of Arabic nations, caused many firms to require added working capital and consumers to consent to sink, even if grudgingly, more deeply into debt. Then prices on the whole began to rise at an unprecedented rate with resulting rises in capital values that made debts seem of little or no burden. Actually many astute observers began to talk about "negative real interest rates," since the rise in a property's value commonly more than covered its original cost and the cost of the interest on funds that had been borrowed to purchase it. If after a lapse of time one could sell durables for more than they cost plus the interest (even though high) on that purchase price, it seemed wise for one to borrow heavily and to buy goods on which to speculate. Perhaps the majority of borrowers, domestic as well as foreign, became very willing debtors. Since many bankers in the U.S. found their firms flush with O.P.E.C. deposits which largely seemed to lie idle and on which likely some interest was being paid, they were eager to lend what they regarded as excess funds to governments and nationals of less-developed countries. The borrowers, including governments in those nations with rising debts, often used such funds to buy new capital goods, expecting to expand output, sales, and exports. Hence debts often seemed to promise self-liquidation.

For diverse reasons, only one of which is the dwindling of the general rises of prices, and particularly the price of petroleum, in the U.S. the era of "negative rates of real interest" has come virtually to an end. Actually, petroleum prices have fallen significantly from their peak. And "double digit" rates of interest have become very heavy burdens on many debtors, foreign and domestic.

However, during that span in the 1970s when our southern trading partners were rushing deeper and deeper into debt to our U.S. banks, the amount of money buyers, especially those in Latin America but also in less industrialized areas elsewhere in the world, were able to spend for imports was distinctly more than what they received as incomes from export of their products. They sold mainly basic raw materials and agricultural goods on which they concentrate. And they bought armaments and capital goods and manufactured consumer goods produced in the U.S., western Europe, Japan, Hong Kong, et cetera. Sellers in our leading free enterprise nations were enabled to "sell dear" and to record handsome money profits, even while our importers were able to "buy cheap," in our trade with less industrially developed nations, particularly those throughout much of Latin America. And our lending to them more and more non-saved, bank-created money has gone on and on since World War II and especially during the 1970s. Some of such lending apparently was given nods of approval by various officials of our U.S. government, ostensibly since it was expected that those less-developed areas would be strengthened industrially and would also become bastions against the threat of communism.

Now in the late 1980s total debts owed by Latin America governments and their nationals to banks mainly in the U.S. are reported to bulk to many hundreds of billions while the contracted interest rates remain quite high by historical standards. Yet all seemed to go well and smoothly so long as the added amount being lent exceeded the aggregate of the repayments falling due on principal plus the interest payments that had been contracted.

For one reason or another, the extensions of new loans eventually must dwindle and even come to an end. We need not here bother to establish the causes of curtailment. The effect is all the same whether mostly lenders find themselves unable or unwilling to extend additional non-saved credit or the borrowers find themselves unable or unwilling to sink even more deeply into debt. In any case further lending by U.S. commercial banks to either government or private borrowers in Latin America virtually has ceased. With it profitable trade, especially for our exporters, must dwindle too. Instead, creditor banks now clamor for payment of the contracted installments that aim to reduce the principal of the debts as well as for the contracted periodic payments of the relatively high interest.

Repayment through the originally scheduled installments on principal as well as the net payment of interest due periodically from Latin American governments and nationals to our big banks, major creditors, is proving to be almost impossible. To pay those obligations according to original schedules, our neighbors to our south (being unable to send us gold, coin or bullion) might, until the early 1980s, still "get by" through reliance on U.S. foreign aid. However, our huge federal government deficits now are about to stop that. They seem to have no course left except that of trying to sell an excess of items, in terms of money value, more than they buy, so as to build up a favorable balance. But historically they have been buying more than they have been selling. They have covered the difference by going into debt deeper and deeper to secure the added purchasing power required. If now they cannot or will not sink into debt still further, and still are obligated to make payments that will cover interest in addition to liquidating some of the principal of that accumulated debt, they can succeed only by reversing the balance of trade from that which has been customary. Bank negotiators, including representatives of the International Monetary Fund, have been advising them, even have been pressuring them, to institute added austerity by importing less while exporting more, thus creating for them favorable foreign financial balances. These can be used to pay interest and installments on principal. In the negotiations some "rescheduling" has been provided, with much or all of the interest due being added on to the principal owed. Also in some cases interest rates have been reduced somewhat.

However, the altered arrangements negotiated in many cases on behalf of the creditors by the spokesmen of the banks plus those of the I.M.F. are unlikely to provide any adequate solution to this virtually insoluble problem. If the arrangement negotiated could be made to work, they might rescue the banks and the creditors. However, there are other parties with equally vital concerns:

1. Exporters from the U.S. (and other developed free enterprise nations) whose sales to Latin American buyers would be reduced significantly.

2. Producers in the U.S. (and in other highly developed areas) whose products will come under increased competition at home and abroad if Latin American exports be increased.

3. The common people, the working class people, the lower economic groups, in the debtor nations upon whom virtually the whole of the increased austerity will be pyramided if more be exported from Latin America with little or no increase in total output, or, alternatively, will be required to work harder or longer hours or be more productive. Certainly, they do not share in any increased volume of output. Indeed, some of the leaders in Latin American nations already have prophesied that the burden of more austerity can be expected to eventuate in rebellion.

And the great overhang of the total U.S. federal government debt coupled with its huge and growing annual deficit practically assures that we no longer may be able, even if willing, to increase greatly our foreign aid or to "bail out" our banks. So if the attempt to collect those bank loans does precipitate rebellion, we ought not blame the situation on communism nor strive to suppress the rebels by advising or aiding military action against them; let one ponder the first few paragraphs of our Declaration of Independence. In order to forestall rebellion in numerous parts of Latin America it is essential that without delay we change our chrematistic system enough that we in this leading free enterprise, mercantilistic nation cease victimizing our fellow men in less-developed lands.

Indeed it appears that, under the guise of free enterprise and *laissez faire,* we may have evolved, unwittingly to be sure, a highly devilish and evil "vicious circle." We may have created through an almost natural, imperceptible, unplanned and unintended process a system of objectives and methods which has caused our neighbors to the south to fall deeper and deeper into our debt. We have pressed them to pay up and have insisted upon their practicing even greater austerity beyond their already relatively low standard. Almost all increased austerity is pyramided eventually on their lower economic classes. That, in turn, gives rise to further discontent and often eventuates in rebellion. Obviously some or many of the rebels claim to favor the only alternative to our capitalism of which they ever have heard, namely communism. But since we champion capitalism and feel threatened seriously by any advocacy of communism (which in time would be aided, of course, by the U.S.S.R.), we may proclaim the need and claim the right to intercede militarily to put down the rebellion and to preserve capitalistic institutions in *their* land. As a consequence of such military action we can hope to preserve for a bit longer our brand of capitalistic free enterprise and puff up our debt-inflation somewhat further. However, sooner or later our whole stack of artificially created prosperity must come tumbling down about us and around us, unless — unless we scurry around with vigor and openmindedness to find and install alterations. Effective changes must be based on the relevant diagnosis and obviate the need for artificial financial expansions as the machinery the workings of which makes big[1] business appear prosperous.

However, rebellion in those Latin American nations whose governments and nationals are deeply in debt to U.S. banks likely is not so imminent and threatening as the prior paragraph may seem to imply. The other parties at interest here in our United States may intercede sufficiently strongly as to prevent the austerity recently agreed upon. Also the political leaders in those debtor countries may resist, too. True increase in austerity surely would involve reduction in our U.S. exports. Our exporters may refuse to permit this and may take political action to prevent it. True increase in austerity in Latin America that would eventuate in favorable balances which can be used by them to pay interest on their debts and reduce significantly the principal owed surely will eventuate in increasing imports into the U.S. (such as textiles from Brazil) which will be resisted here by our domestic manufacturers. Also our manufacturers will encounter increased competition in striving to make sales in other nations. Those who are in political authority (or who may attain such authority by election) in Latin American nations likely will refuse to let austerity be pushed so far so to spark rebellion; some already have expressed fear of this danger and some have asserted their resolve to place limits of one sort or another on the amount or rate of net payment on the interest and principal of their debts.

[1]   Attention in Ch.9 is confined to "big" free enterprise firms because virtually every one of them has absentee-owners and, to be successful, must record profits, of the type required by corporate law and corporate accounting, from which dividends thereafter can be distributed to those absentee-owners. In contrast "little" free enterprise firms (being 97% or a bit more of all producer entities in the U.S. doing, however, not more than 25% of total production) overwhelmingly can "succeed" without making profits of that corporate-law and corporate-accounting type, since their owners usually participate as workers or as managers and right out of the firms' capital funds are paid wages and/or salaries that are adequate rewards to keep those ventures functioning. If every firm were a little one and competition always thoroughgoing, Adam Smith's *laissez faire* might be made to work, but fully developed division of labor makes that impracticable.

Also, it is possible that a few of our neighbor nations south of the U.S. may find their situations improved and themselves able to meet their debt obligations in a halting fashion, especially if there be some scaling down of the rate of interest and some stretching out of maturity dates. For example, Brazil, which is reported to have used much of its borrowings to enlarge and modernize its productive capacity of textiles, might be able to export enough output to remain "solvent" and even current on its debt — if U.S. import duties on textiles are not increased and such items from the southern hemisphere can be turned out competitively with Hong Kong, Korea, and the two Chinas. If the price of crude petroleum continues the modest increase that currently (early 1985) can be observed, Mexico may be able to meet a softened schedule of payments.

As indicated in the title of this chapter, Japan, and some other political entities during these last several years, seem to have "turned the tables" on the United States and may be reducing us essentially to colonial status. Other lesser entities that seem to be "beating us at our own game" include Hong Kong, Singapore, South Korea, Taiwan, West Germany, and possibly several Arabian countries. Let attention be focused on Japan, even though similar observations may apply elsewhere. Japan now is outdoing the U.S. in numerous important lines of manufacturing, and year by year is selling here many billions of dollars' worth more of products than they purchase from us. They have enjoyed a huge favorable balance of trade from us year by year in each of the last several years. Obviously we in the U.S. have been "suffering unfavorable trade balances" that correspond.

The Japanese, apparently by offering employment security to their workers as well as by using much automation and new, more modern plants and equipment (often copied later from experience here in the U.S. and in western Europe), have been able to pay much lower production wages and to turn out high quality goods. They have been outproducing us and underselling us in many lines of smokestack industries and more recently in electronics. To outdo us they need simply to continue to hold down their unit costs in such lines.

Further, the Japanese, along with smaller competitors of ours, regard the U.S. monetary unit as especially strong. They are glad to receive dollars in considerable excess and to accumulate them, likely often as deposits to their credit in U.S. banks as well as in their own banks. And they are glad to "invest" some of their "favorable balance" (against us) by buying up a portion of our federal government obligations and often, too, by buying up in the U.S. land and production facilities and equipment and financial institutions as well as some pieces of housing property, recreation and vacation real estate and facilities.

Indeed the amount of real and personal property that is coming to be owned by the Japanese and by governments and firms and nationals headquartered abroad, and the amount of the debt we now owe abroad, including the U.S. government debt held by foreigners, is or ought to be viewed with considerable concern by us. Before long we may be in the position of a colony, vassals to those in other lands.

Incidentally, some readers may find it interesting and useful to note that the insights disclosed herein naturally imply that much of the history of the Western World during the modern era ought to be given a chrematistic interpretation (in contrast to an "economic interpretation"). A huge portion of our political and military actions ought to be viewed in terms of big business striving to "make money." Other forces have been responsible for political, diplomatic, and military actions, too, such as religion and, to a more minor extent, the ambition for power by a variety of individuals or groups. However, actual production and exchange and distribution of goods and services devoted to helping to satisfy human wants has been during the last four or more centuries far less important in explaining political and diplomatic and military history than has the drive of big firms to earn and record money profits. The latter has dominated such actions both in the Classical Period of Mercantilism and the period of reliance principally on debt-inflation these last few hundreds of years.

(This chapter is closed, as it began, with a cry for help. Many insights here require without question to be altered and corrected, expanded, and perfected. Adequate time is no longer available for me to do the job alone. My competence is insufficient in certain languages and knowledge of the facts and statistical information that apply. Good analysts who can be objective and who have grasp of the fundamentals of the naturally evolved money-making objective of big [producing] business firms can aid in perfecting the diagnosis as it actually operates in connection with the less fully industrialized areas of the world.)

CHAPTER 10

We, The U.S.A. and the U.S.S.R., Together Can Forestall Armageddon

One great benefit of having made understandable the congenital defect in the financial objective and methods of big producing firms in the highly developed free enterprise portions of this world is that a superhighway has been opened to institute changes that can yield harmony rather than confrontation. We in the U.S. now readily can find, develop, and install changes, those which are relevant prescriptions of medication, and/or surgery, and/or therapy that will enable our free enterprise system for producing and distributing goods and services to function in a greatly improved and acceptable manner. And the U.S.S.R., in a similar manner, also can identify flaws in its system and set about devising specific alterations that will improve the functioning of its processes for satisfying wants. Each of us first must look inward. We must find our shortcomings, our flaws, and failures and must ascertain and install the specific treatment for each ailment that will improve economic and financial health. Note that what is being described is constructive change little-by-little, not simply any broad and general condemnation and certainly not the complete displacement of an existing system with a different, untried, and unproved theoretical alternative. Since a great new scheme almost never functions as well as its advocates theorize as they press for its adoption, we shall make far more satisfactory and successful progress by correctly identifying and isolating each specific flaw and then developing the indicated prescription for overcoming that. We will cure the ailment if possible, but at least we will find the treatment that will reduce its detrimental effects, avoid its serious harm and be able to "live with it."

My prediction is that, if we in the U.S.A. really do choose leaders who concentrate on finding and curing (or counteracting) the flaws in our own system, including those identified herein, and if the people in the U.S.S.R. are led to concentrate similarly on finding and correcting the flaws in their system, we shall discover very soon that our two (purportedly divergent) systems will grow more and more alike. We shall become increasingly willing to learn from each other and to copy some of the best features from the other system. Our friendship will grow.

That which each of our two systems needs quite urgently is a leader at the top who has great wisdom, and who surrounds himself with advisers of great wisdom. Such a leader should be easy to identify. He must be one who, while possessed of the normal qualifications of leadership, is fearlessly sure of the fallibility of institutions of the production and financial system of his nation and of his own insights concerning the capitalistic or the communistic system he leads. He must be fearless in the quest by himself and by his advisers to find the flaws in his nation's system, to perfect the diagnosis of that system's illnesses. He must devise the specific prescription that will counteract or cure each malady, one by one. He will insist that the shortcomings of the production and financial system he leads are corrected before he will let his nation be driven or enticed into starting any military action in an effort to maintain his nation's production and financial institutions unchanged. My prior prediction deserves to be repeated. When a sufficiently wise leader has made certain that the flaws in our capitalistic system here in the U.S.A. have been corrected or counteracted and a similarly wise leader in the U.S.S.R. has made certain that the flaws in his communistic system are correct- ed or counteracted, our two systems will be much more alike than at present. Our two nations will have advanced far along the road to friendship. As a by-product, less-developed lands will be greatly benefited in a number of ways. War, especially nuclear action, will become less and less likely.

It is not in any way being suggested that the U.S.A. and the U.S.S.R. should hasten first to disarm. Disarmament will follow, to the extent that seems wise, after each of us has made sincere progress in overcoming the flaws in his own system. But it will be useful for our two nations to agree in the meantime to freeze various kinds of weapons at what now seems adequate deterrence on each side. It is, of course, impossible to make any close com- parisons as to parity because of our divergent military instru- ments. Further, we wisely should delay actual reduction of existing arms pending our making sure that other governments, elsewhere in the world, have been enticed by our examples to improve their own systems of production and finance so they can feel content to refrain from starting military action, especially against their neighbors. Then they can provide increased human liberty and freedom and democracy at home.

When one has diagnosed at last the efficient cause of an ailment, as herein the nature and process of overall profit-making in the macrochrematistics sense by our big producer firms, it is to be expected that he who makes the discovery will generate some ideas as to relevant prescription(s). Such is the case, of course, in the present instance. The temptation is very great for such a one to rush on to describe those ideas regarding proper treatment.

However, that temptation is largely being resisted; but a few comments will be offered primarily as illustrations and stimulations. Note that it will please me greatly later, after my diagnosis has been fully and objectively evaluated, and hopefully perfected and verified, to set forth in one or more "brainstorming" sessions composed of competent and objective associates the suggested prescriptions my analyses have generated.

As a first illustration of an improvement that can be offered, consider the production system of the U.S.S.R. There is at least one aspect in which the Soviet system is greatly superior to our Western capitalistic system, namely, in providing job security. We in the U.S., and in other leading capitalistic nations, keep violating one of the most basic of human rights, that of economic security and a continuous right to earn a living by everyone willing and able to work. This is not only during depressions, but now on a large scale in what we struggle to label as reasonable prosperity. The truly communistic nations avoid any need to worry about unemployment. Even in their isolated labor camps, the Soviets now may treat their citizens no worse than we in our nation treated our slaves a few generations past and no worse than we treat our Indian survivors even today as well as many of our unemployed, and especially our non-white citizens. But all citizens in the U.S.S.R. (and apparently in other communistic areas) evidently are assured of jobs and economic security if they are willing to work, even though their average standard of living may be low by comparison with ours.

Further, it appears that the communistic system of the U.S.S.R. is far superior to our capitalistic system in that it avoids financial spasms. Our depressions descend upon us quite irregularly, since we have moved to the technique of bank-money creation devoid of any requirement for redemption in any money of substance. We may put off the "day of reckoning" a bit longer — while we rush on to entangle our finances into a larger and more puzzling mess. Unless we make some changes, that evil day undoubtedly will come again, after only a few years' delay at the very longest.

Again, it appears that the Soviet system may prove to be superior to ours in that it is less in danger of internal rebellion. Should we suffer a very serious depression (my prediction is of a forthcoming depression far greater than that of 1929 and the early 1930s unless we very soon perfect and institute the indicated corrective treatments) we shall be confronted with rebellion as unemployment grows to an unbearable number, unemployment which the federal government no longer seems able to relieve. Here in the U.S.A. any rebellion will be against the wealthy and those with big incomes or those entrenched in positions of security and ease. But in the U.S.S.R. there is not likely to be a depression and not likely to be any serious unemployment. There apparently exists no group of really wealthy persons with entrenched privileges and security against whom to rebel. How could a rebellion occur and against whom? True, a group, such as the Solidarity Union in Poland, might demand higher wages and shorter hours and lower prices. However, if such a group does come to power, how would they raise wages or shorten the hours of work or reduce the prices of goods and services (unless they subjugate and press down still further a great mass of people in the very lowest economic class)?

While the Soviet system provides economic security for all in the sense of employment (hence some purchasing power) for everyone able and willing to work, and the disparity between wealth ownership among its people and between the sizes of their incomes is not great, but their system does have flaws that they should strive to correct. The most evident flaw, it seems to me, is the lack of adequate incentive to induce its citizens to be highly productive. That is the same shortcoming that the first English colony (intended to be permanent) in America encountered when communism of a sort was tried there. It is reported that before the lapse of much time Captain John Smith, who was in command at

Jamestown, Virginia, found it necessary to decree that "He who doesn't work, shan't eat." In other words, when everyone is expected to share the results of his efforts about equally with all others, the great majority of people are likely to become careless and laggard in their assigned tasks. It is much easier and perhaps almost natural to let others perform the labor if there be little or no relationship between one's own productivity and his standard of living or his accumulation of wealth. In a true communistic system there usually can be expected to be almost no inventiveness or ingenuity or innovation. It is much easier simply to "ride along." There can be expected to be almost no widespread genuine drive to be as efficient and productive as possible. Since output tends to remain minimal and since all persons tend to share approximately alike, what they do, and continue to do, is to share the shortages caused by lack of incentive to be as ingenious and as productive as possible.

Should the leaders in the U.S.S.R. ever truly find the key to provide the incentive to make the vast majority of their people inventive and innovative and highly efficient and productive, they actually might almost succeed in a boast of more than two decades past to "bury us." They need not worry, as now we must, about our unemployment during what is proclaimed to be a "prosperous period" here, let alone the great added unemployment of any forthcoming capitalistic depression. A super-depression seems imminent in view of our imponderable financial tangles, which keep growing worse and worse.

To help overcome the flaw that appears so obvious and so persistent in the communistic system of the U.S.S.R., it is my suggestion that there be experimentation in that nation with the use of some portions of private enterprise as we know it in the U.S. Slightly modified forms of individual proprietorships and partnerships, patterned after those under Anglo-American law, should be permitted. Note carefully that corporation forms of organization are strictly omitted from the above. Some additional modifications to our proprietorship and partnership institutions to make them useful in the U.S.S.R. are the following:

1. Such a permitted private venture should be required to engage in production which can be in creation of time or place or ownership utilities, as well as creation of form utilities.

2. It should be permitted to own outright only a small parcel of land, if any. It might be permitted to rent land needed for its production purposes and for as long as normally required to engage in efficient production.

3. Private ownership of non-renewable resources should not be permitted. But use and development of such resources should be subject to special contract with the government, wherein title actually resides.

4. Earnings should be subject to graduated income taxes that still preserve rewards, if earned, sufficient to maintain incentives, but prevent great accumulations of private wealth.

5. Estate and/or inheritance taxes should be sufficient to prevent any great accumulations of private wealth.

6. If a partnership, each partner should be required to be active in the firm, and there should be no limited or secret partners, and each should have individually full liability for all debts of the firm. However, partners should be permitted to adopt by contract whatever terms and arrangement they desire to govern their financial obligations to each other.

7. Any individual as a sole proprietor or the partners in a partnership should be permitted to draw compensation for themselves out of the capital funds of the enterprise without need

first to sell products for more than the latter's cost and expenses. This can be done so long as done openly and creditors can be sure that they are not wrongfully endangered.

8. Laws and regulations should be installed as needed to assure that these private business operations are legal, highly ethical, and just.

Let attention be returned now to a consideration of business corporations. Since Adam Smith was unqualifiedly critical of and opposed to corporations and advocated their eradication, it follows that should the Soviet Union experiment with private proprietorships and partnerships, along the lines suggested above, it will be adopting for such trial much of the *laissez-faire* system that Smith had in mind. The U.S.S.R. should not hesitate to try this, even though in doing so they will move definitely in the direction of being *a bit* like the U.S.A. and other leading capitalistic nations. It might go a long way towards solving at least one problem that appears to be a flaw in their system. The Soviets might obtain some help or advice from China which is already experimenting along the same path. Perhaps the Soviets and the Chinese will both benefit and improve their friendship, too.

But more deserves to be said about business corporations, such as those evolved in the U.S.A. Some of the following comments will be found to favor them and some comments will be found critical of them. First, it merits repeating that Adam Smith, the champion of *laissez-faire* free enterprise, was unqualifiedly opposed to business corporations, what few of them existed in his era. He criticized them so thoroughly as to recommend their eradication. Hence any person who now strives to advocate free enterprise and purports to be a follower of Adam Smith should feel compelled to renounce privately owned corporations, otherwise he will prostitute what was the historic initial position of *laissez faire.*

However, in fairness to Smith, it should be realized that those few business corporations chartered by the sovereign that did exist in his era were virtually all created as monopolies. Each of them was authorized to carry on exclusive trade with a designated foreign area. Additional corporations, likely much more numerous than the few engaged in foreign trade, were created by municipal authority as organizations each made up of master craftsmen in a particular trade and authorized to regulate the production and commerce of that trade. Each of them tended to make rules to govern and to limit the manufacture and sale of its specialized products. Limitations on the number of apprentices each master craftman could employ and the term of apprenticeship were especially popular. Of course Adam Smith regarded all corporations as being monopolistic, and condemned them accordingly.

There are insufficient grounds for speculating how Smith might evaluate business corporations now, some two centuries later. There is little benefit in anyone now trying to draw more than a few broad conclusions on the matter. But one expectation does seem thoroughly clear. Adam Smith's brand of *laissez faire* was meant by him to apply to natural human beings. It was people, people capable of being citizens and not artificially created entities, that were to be let alone and permitted to seek their own best good in carrying on economic and financial activities.

In quite recent times here in the U.S.A. some argument has arisen as to how properly to interpret the Constitution of this nation. But no one has any ground to argue that in that document business corporations were intended by its framers to have the rights of natural human beings, of full citizens, for there existed almost no business corporations here in the new United States of America in 1776, nor in 1787. If our Constitution were intended to embody the *laissez faire* arrangement advocated by Adam Smith, then corporations deserved instead to be eradicated. Too, the framers of our Constitution could not possibly have intended to be in favor of banking corporations that can exercise the power of creating money. The money-creating process was not even fully comprehended until the mid-1850s when H. D. Mcleod's book on the theory and practice of banking was published. Those who formulated our underlying, fundamental law were completely specific in delegating to Congress the power to coin money and to regulate its value. Furthermore, many of those who authored our Constitution helped legislate and launch in 1791 our First Bank of the United States, the main purpose of which was to prevent private banks that were springing up from issuing a lot of their own bank notes. That bank was directed continuously to require such notes to be redeemed in standard coin. One interesting added comment is that the First Bank of the United States was given a charter for only twenty years which was allowed to expire at the conclusion of that period. Our Congress in 1791 and in 1811 did not wish such a corporation to take on a life of its own.

In the paragraphs that follow are sketched some possible constructive changes needed to enable free-enterprise to survive. But it is *not* suggested by me to any brainstorming session that business corporations ought to be eliminated nor even that money-creating privately owned banks, though their activities have been highly detrimental by eventuating nearly invariably in debt-inflation and then depression, should all be wiped out. On the one hand it has not been possible for me to conjure up any substitute form of organization that will meet the need in numerous cases for such large-scale enterprise as to make possible the full development of division of labor and the realization of the maximum benefits of the economies of scale. And on the other hand a mere wiping out now the money supply that has been created by our banking system would bring on complete financial chaos. Free enterprise might never recover, and even if it did survive a long interval of serious depression the many-sided chaos would be devastating almost beyond imagination.

Since the money-creating processes must be reformed if the fundamentals and benefits of capitalistic free enterprise can avoid demise, let a suggestion for constructive change of commercial banking be offered as an illustration to stimulate thinking by any brainstorming session, while yet recognizing that other changes (such as with respect to the money-making objective of big business) also will be required. Accordingly this generalized illustrative change is sketched for consideration by brainstormers as something that might be beneficial (but some other attack might, of course, be found superior): Every banking entity that issues bank notes (intended to circulate as hand-to-hand money) or has demand deposits subject to checks or negotiable-orders-of-withdrawal or any activities that in any way eventuate in the creation of money, shall be limited to engaging in commercial banking types of operations only, having no deposits except demand deposit subject to checks, and shall divest itself of all other kinds of operations not related to money creation. (There is a variety of processes by which a banking firm can divest itself of other types of operations; these include, but are not limited to, the transfer of other kinds of liabilities and corresponding assets to a holding company of which it remains an affiliate.) Its deposits shall be solely demand deposits subject to checks. And no interest shall be paid on deposits of any sort. Its deposits (being demand deposits only) shall be frozen in amount at the maximum they have attained on a specified base date, perhaps a recent date in the past, and each commercial banking firm shall be permitted to renew old loans and make new loans to maintain its deposits at such permitted maximum, except that the total deposits held by any such bank (each bank considered separately) shall be permitted to increase by the same amount that it holds of greenbacks in its own vault beyond those greenbacks held by it on the specified base date. The U.S. federal government shall issue additional greenbacks, period by period, sufficient to keep the whole money supply in "circulation," including those greenbacks held in bank vaults, increasing in the same ratio that the nation's population increases.

It seems likely that many people will oppose the adoption of the changes offered for consideration to stimulate various groups of brainstormers in their quests to find the most constructive alterations. At the moment of writing, probably the vast majority of bankers will object, many violently. But the foregoing ideas, one possible line of alteration, are offered as a choice among evils. Choosing to install changes along the lines that have been sketched is intended to save the existing banks from a far worse fate. If we continue with our banking institutions just as they now are and let them function as they have been, my prediction, repeated, is that before long, and likely sooner rather than later, we shall encounter a still worse financial depression and that money-creating banks will be wiped out nearly in whole. And that will prove to be a sad, possibly a fatal, day for the free enterprise system as we have known it. It is my hope to endure long enough to see some important reforms made as a result of my chrematistic analysis designed to preserve the beneficial aspects of the free enterprise system, and forestall the depression otherwise likely to befall us.

Some reforms or changes ought to be weighed as stimulants to participants in brainstorming sessions to help them perfect diagnoses of defects and shortcomings in our capitalistic free enterprise systems and to prescribe successfully for countering or curing those maladies that vigorous and objective analyses disclose. A congenital defect in business corporations (not inevitably true of sole proprietorships or partnerships), in free enterprise capitalism as we know it, revealed and explained here, is that by naturally evolved custom and by the accounting precepts that developed and by the legal restraints that followed later, all of these have required that producing corporate firms in order to pay dividend-rewards to owners first must sell items of output for prices which on the whole exceed the costs and expenses attributed to the goods and services sold. That requirement, in order to be realized in the overall or macro-chrematistic sense, has come to rely during the last two centuries mainly on expansion of the money in circulation as provided in our time principally by money-creating banking. If free enterprise is to survive the straightening out of the imponderable financial tangle now so exasperating in the U.S.A., the nature of paying rewards to business corporate equity owners must be changed. Here is offered the suggestion for consideration in brainstorming conferences the general proposal that reasonable rewards to equity owners be made actual costs or expenses of production and paid, along with other costs, say quarterly or semi-annually, right out of capital funds. Various alternatives might be used to make this possible. The law that prohibits distribution of corporate dividends out of capital funds and the accounting precepts applicable could be amended to make such reasonable payments permissible and desirable. Or subordinate debenture bonds of a total value equal to the fair capital value of prudent investment in a firm might be distributed pro rata to the owners of stock. Or subordinate debenture bonds with voting rights might be issued exclusively and all stock issues retired by exchange or omitted in starting a new firm. A base amount of 8% or 10% annually should be permitted to be distributed in periodic installments. The purpose is to distribute to the final owners of the equity some such percentage on the fair capital value of prudent investment as part of the costs of production. The aim is to obviate the need for producing firms to first earn and record profits by antecedently selling items of output at money prices greater than the money costs and expenses incurred.

Some such simple and almost painless change can be adequately constructive in prescribing successful treatment or surgery for the congenital defect of the capitalistic system of production.

Further, since any corporation might make a considerable money profit beyond all costs and expenses, including the rewards for equity owners described in the preceding paragraph, there ought to be provision for each firm with such extra earnings to pay "income" tax on those earnings. The "income" (profits) tax should be graduated and rise eventually to a very high rate. There can be asserted several justifications for such taxation of the extra profits of any corporation. First, since on the whole corporate profits can no longer be generated through an increase in the supply of money circulating, it will cause those who garner a great amount extra to turn much of that extra over to government which will put the money back into circulation promptly, of course. Second, it will minimize the temptation for the management of any firm to strive, using sharp, unethical, or illegal practices, to help it grow large beyond that size which attains the full advantages of division of labor and economies of scale. Thus, it will help preserve competition. Further, if the tax rate on lower brackets is small, that will help young firms to enjoy hastened growth toward maturity. Again, it will help compensate the government that has created it; hence it will help pay citizens for some of the great advantages it enjoys as the results of their having given it birth. Although there surely are other justifications for steeply graduated tax on corporation net profits, as offered here for consideration, those mentioned above seem sufficient.

As a final suggestion offered to stimulate thinking, it is my belief that we wisely must place a great added obligation on business corporations since we must institute constructive changes that will forestall the gigantic depression that our puzzling and knotty financial tangle presages. Or, instead, we must be prepared to help our free enterprise system recover if we begin to suffer that depression which seems so likely. If we are unsuccessful with both the forestalling and the managing of a smooth recovery, it seems likely that our system of corporations as well as our money-creating banks all will "go under" and be eliminated. Obviously corporations have much to lose, since they have great strength and power. Indeed a business corporation often serves as a supreme example of a whole that is far greater than the sum of its parts. It is ten, a hundred, or even a thousand times more powerful than the individuals to whom the charter is granted by sovereign authority. Accordingly, it is right and just that business corporations be charged with certain special obligations, such as steeply graduated taxes on profits. Because of a corporation's greatly multiplied power, a tax on corporate profits is not simply a tax on stockholders and not truly double taxation.

Accordingly, this is the special obligation offered here for brainstorming consideration: Although a business corporation shall be permitted by a specific agreement to employ a worker temporarily for, say, not more than two months and shall incur no further obligation, if his employment extends beyond two months that worker shall be entitled to job security. However, he can be dismissed at any time due to a sufficient failure on his part (i.e., for a "just cause"), which accusation of failure shall be subject to appeal and a proper hearing. It appears that this is essentially what the Japanese private firms are already doing with some government help. We might be well advised to confer with the Japanese and adopt, with some modifications, the best features of their institutions.

Indeed, this suggestion that business corporations be obligated to supply job security for their workers might even be made somewhat retroactive in application, especially if a very serious depression does descend upon us before we succeed in adopting those changes which will overcome our existing financial deficiencies. The "price" business corporations will pay may be large. Yet it may be far less than the extreme penalty that it seems probable will descend upon them if a huge amount of unemployment results, for great unemployment may be even more than our governments, already saddled with huge debts, may be able to alleviate. There is high likelihood that corporations may face a choice between what their owners may regard as two evils, namely, either provide job security for their workers (thus keeping the latter somewhat satisfied) or be wiped out as a result of overpowering discontent brought on by extremely deep depression and unbearable unemployment.

To correct our existing flaws and counter the great harm that severe depression is apt to create, the workers themselves undoubtedly must pay a "price" too. In exchange for job security, although each worker must be permitted the right to quit his job at any time, he should be denied the right to strike in concert and agreement with fellow workers, such a strike being held to be legally a conspiracy (as long was the case in the history of the U.S.A.).

Each business corporation, in return for job security extended to its workers, should be given the right to reduce wage rates as needed in order to maintain its solvency and viability, but with several limitations. Consider the following:

1. No salary plus bonuses plus any other personnel compensation paid to an executive or a supervisor shall exceed twenty times the average wage (plus bonuses) paid in the same year to non-executive and non-supervisory employees.

2. Total salaries plus bonuses and personnel compensation paid to executives and supervisors in any year shall not exceed 15% (brainstormers may find a more valid number) as much as the compensation paid to other workers collectively in the same year.

3. If the average wage and other personnel compensation to non-executive and non-supervisory workers be reduced, the

whole year being considered, the reward to equity owners that is payable out of capital funds shall be reduced by the same ratio. If the latter was 10% on fair capital value and if worker compensation is reduced by 15%, then the allowable payment to owners permissible out of capital funds would drop to 8.5%.

4. If the average wage or other personnel compensation to workers is raised, either the average worker compensation rate or the total compensation to workers collectively, the payment to owners permissible out of capital funds may be raised at the same rate or even at a bit higher ratio.

5. With respect to what profit might be left in any large corporation's accounting records after the disbursements of money to owners and executives and supervisors and workers in those ways specified above, steeply progressive "income" taxes shall be applied. The objectives are, on the one hand, to enable small, growing firms rapidly to gain maturity, and on the other hand, to prevent mature firms, already sufficiently large, from taking full advantage of the best division of labor simply to enrich a few people. Extreme gaps in wealth ownership or in incomes seem always to provide fertile soil in which to grow trouble.

Adoption of the fundamentals of changes as sketched in the last few paragraphs will cause corporations in our capitalistic, free enterprise system to develop characteristics which are in certain respects somewhat like the production communes of the U.S.S.R.

In the course of brainstorming in diagnosing the defects in our capitalistic free enterprise system and its functioning, it is hoped that careful attention will be given to what can be learned from the study of "a bonus system" to augment worker compensation, such as that long used by the Lincoln Electric Company of Cleveland, Ohio.

Any group that chooses can engage in the brainstorming, and ought to be encouraged to do so. It seems imperative that the U.S.A. and the U.S.S.R. should each officially create a group charged with undertaking the brainstorming that has been described. Further, it would be wise if it could be arranged that not less frequently than once every few months a small group of the leading "official" brainstormers from each of our two nations hold a joint session, being charged not to condemn each other, but to aid each other. From time to time, similarly charged brainstormers from China and Japan should be invited to participate, too. China has been experimenting with some non-corporate free enterprise and can supply revealing experiences. Japan is reported to provide, either by law or by custom, that each business firm be responsible for a large measure of job security for its workers. Certain leading Latin American countries should be invited to send small delegations, too. They can be regarded as "associate" members as also may participants from other nations. Invariably the charge on everyone must be that, by brainstorming, all will labor to find, one by one, specific shortcomings in one's own and in each other's economic and chrematistic system. They must find the indicated prescriptions that will cure or alleviate the malady diagnosed. If brainstormers from two or more nations hold joint sessions, there yet should be no formal organization beyond that which is merely sufficient to assure orderly meetings. Fault-finding should be confined to identifying and diagnosing specific flaws. Each person who alleges the existence of a flaw in the economic or financial or chrematistic system of his own or another nation shall be obligated to describe what he believes may be the most useful prescription of successful treatment. Finally, publication of any sort of report by any of the participants should be left for action as each national group may choose.

For solid emphasis this paragraph is added as a postscript. It urges as their duty those who undertake to devise improvements that will assure the survival of the underlying great benefits of the free enterprise system (typified by the economy of the U.S.) as well as those who strive to improve the functioning of the communistic system (typified by the economy of the U.S.S.R.) that they always hold in the forefront of their thinking two most fundamental objectives. Those objectives are, in changing each system likely by gradual steps, to (1) provide and maintain great, even universal, incentives which will stimulate innovations that will improve and augment production technically, and also (2) remove financial institutions forever from acting as any sort of restraint on production. We must make sure that output of goods and services as well as employment will proceed without interruption at the maximum sustainable level of capacity. The money system and the financial system must be caused to serve simply and essentially as facilitators. Our economies worldwide must be altered in ways that will lead them to operate basically as the underlying premise of Say's Law erroneously has assumed that they always do; they must furnish through cost and expense payments (of which corporate dividend distributions now in fact are not a part) to those who participate in the production of goods and services (the creation of time and place and ownership utilities as well as form creation) aggregate purchasing power (via incomes) that will equal the value of the entire output. Such income recipients must be empowered to acquire their shares of want-satisfying products without going into debt (collectively speaking, since saving and lending out of incomes and repaying out of incomes often is desirable and to be encouraged). Incidentally, as we must make employment secure as well as rewarding; these can be expected as ready by-products of the attainment of the two numbered objectives listed above.

Meanwhile, if key financial institutions are not altered promptly, the worldwide artificial prosperity of free enterprise big business likely will accelerate its climb to some still greater height, from which before long it will fall.

Index

G

Garcia, Alan . . . Perez, 18
General Theory of Employment, Interest and Money, The, ii, 21, 100-101
Germany, western, 113
Gilder, George, ii, 24 ,101-102
G. N. P., 39
Goldsmiths, 64 *et seq.* 74, 123 *et seq.*

I

Increased capital value
    borrowing against, 96-97
Indexation pump, The, 18, 94
Institute of the Americas, 142-143
Institutionalists, 34
Inventory accumulation, effect of, 80

J

Japan (and others) reducing U.S.A. to colonial status, 152-154, 172

K

Keynes, John M., ii, 21, 23, 100-101, 134

L

Latin American countries, 11, 18, 142, 147 *et seq.*
Law, John, 77, 132

R

S

T

U

V